Cooking Light
LUNCH TO GO
recipes • hints • tips

Oxmoor House®

Mr. Stripey Tomato, Arugula,
and Pancetta Sandwiches, page 52

Welcome

If you're a busy mom, student, or worker bee, or if you admit to frequenting the vending machine or spending way too much for lunches out that never truly satisfy, then *Cooking Light Eat Smart Guide: Lunch To Go* is your ticket to midday meals you'll look forward to and feel good about.

Packing lunch can get monotonous. If you tire of the same old sandwich or salad and find yourself in a brown-bag rut, *Cooking Light Eat Smart Guide: Lunch To Go* was created just for you. This go-to guide is chock-full of information and practical advice for those wanting to look forward to their lunch breaks again.

Loaded with tantalizing options that can be put together with ease and will surely please all ages and appetites, this book will teach you how to stock your pantry and fridge; prepare foods for portability; and focus on eating healthy, delicious foods that will sustain you through hectic afternoons whether you're at work, in study hall, or shuttling kids to and from activities.

Cooking Light Eat Smart Guide: Lunch To Go is all about simplicity and dishes that travel well and taste great whenever you're ready to have a bite. Whether you're packing for a picnic under the stars or a field trip to the zoo, we guarantee recipe success and satisfaction. Coming from the most respected cooking authority in America, you can trust these 80 recipes to work, taste great, and come with a detailed nutritional analysis so you can make choices that suit your lifestyle. It's time to put an end to brown-bagging boredom forever!

The *Cooking Light* Editors

ISBN-13: 978-0-8487-3306-3
ISBN-10: 0-8487-3306-1
Library of Congress Control Number: 2009937181
Printed in the United States of America
First printing 2010

Be sure to check with your health-care provider before making any changes in your diet.

OXMOOR HOUSE
VP, Publishing Director: Jim Childs
Editorial Director: Susan Payne Dobbs
Brand Manager: Michelle Turner Aycock
Senior Editor: Heather Averett
Managing Editor: Laurie S. Herr

Cooking Light® Eat Smart Guide: Lunch To Go

Editor: Katherine Cobbs
Project Editor: Diane Rose
Senior Designer: Emily Albright Parrish
Director, Test Kitchens: Elizabeth Tyler Austin
Assistant Director, Test Kitchens:
  Julie Christopher
Test Kitchens Professionals:
  Allison E. Cox, Julie Gunter,
  Kathleen Royal Phillips,
  Catherine Crowell Steele,
  Ashley T. Strickland
Photography Director: Jim Bathie
Senior Photo Stylist: Kay E. Clarke
Associate Photo Stylist:
  Katherine Eckert Coyne
Production Manager: Theresa Beste-Farley

Contributors
Compositor: Teresa Cole
Copy Editor: Rhonda Richards
Interns: Georgia Dodge, Perri K. Hubbard,
  Christine Taylor

To order additional publications, call 1-800-765-6400 or 1-800-491-0551.

For more books to enrich your life, visit **oxmoorhouse.com**

To search, savor, and share thousands of recipes, visit **myrecipes.com**

Cooking Light®

Editor: Scott Mowbray
Creative Director: Carla Frank
Deputy Editor: Phillip Rhodes
Food Editor: Ann Taylor Pittman
Special Publications Editor: Mary Simpson
  Creel, M.S., R.D.
Nutrition Editor: Kathy Kitchens Downie, R.D.
Associate Food Editors: Timothy Q. Cebula,
  Julianna Grimes
Associate Editors: Cindy Hatcher,
  Brandy Rushing
Test Kitchen Director: Vanessa T. Pruett
Assistant Test Kitchen Director: Tiffany Vickers
Chief Food Stylist: Charlotte Fekete
Senior Food Stylist: Kellie Gerber Kelley
Recipe Testers and Developers:
  Robin Bashinsky, SaBrina Bone,
  Deb Wise
Art Director: Fernande Bondarenko
Deputy Art Director: J. Shay McNamee
Junior Deputy Art Director:
  Alexander Spacher
Designer: Chase Turberville
Photo Director: Kristen Schaefer
Senior Photographer: Randy Mayor
Senior Photo Stylist: Cindy Barr
Photo Stylist: Leigh Ann Ross
Copy Chief: Maria Parker Hopkins
Assistant Copy Chief: Susan Roberts
Research Editor: Michelle Gibson Daniels
Editorial Production Director: Liz Rhoades
Production Editor: Hazel R. Eddins
Art/Production Assistant: Josh Rutledge
Administrative Coordinator: Carol D. Johnson
Cookinglight.com Editor: Allison Long Lowery

Contents

LUNCH TO GO
Fresh
Salads

The Sweet Truth About Bitter Greens

by Mark Bittman

NOT SO LONG AGO, IF YOU SERVED A SALAD MADE WITH BITTER GREENS AND LETTUCES IN PLACE OF ICEBERG, GUESTS MIGHT NOT HAVE UNDERSTOOD. Although arugula, endive, radicchio, sorrel, and watercress have always been popular in Europe, they're just being discovered here. Today, supermarkets across the country feature a year-round profusion of lettuces and greens that were once considered specialty items. Consumption of these greens has exploded since the advent of gourmet packaged salads. Of course, these lettuces and greens aren't just for salads, as our recipes demonstrate. They can stand up to spicy seasonings, aromatic herbs, and tangy dressings, hallmarks of contemporary cooking trends. They even hold their own in a soup or a risotto.

Then there's the health factor, which has also helped boost their appeal. People always knew that greens were good for them—they just didn't realize *how* good. Radicchio and endive are nutritional champs, brimming with vitamin A and iron.

As for versatility, in many cases these greens can be readily substituted for one another. If you want to know just how much eating preferences have changed of late, try serving your guests a plain old iceberg lettuce salad. Considering all the current choices of greens and lettuces filling supermarket produce bins, they might not understand.

Mesclun with Berries and Sweet Spiced Almonds

Raspberries add bright color and several good-for-you nutrients, such as fiber, antioxidants, and vitamin C. Almonds are a good source of vitamin E and monounsaturated fats. Chives, members of the onion family, add phenols and flavonoids.

5 cups gourmet salad greens
1³/₄ cups raspberries (about 1 (6-ounce) container)
¹/₄ cup chopped fresh chives
3 tablespoons champagne vinegar or white wine vinegar
2 teaspoons honey
¹/₂ teaspoon country-style Dijon mustard

¹/₄ teaspoon salt
¹/₈ teaspoon freshly ground black pepper
1 tablespoon canola oil
6 tablespoons Sweet Spiced Almonds, page 11

1. Combine first 3 ingredients in a large bowl. Combine champagne vinegar and next 4 ingredients in a small bowl. Gradually add oil, stirring with a whisk. Drizzle vinegar mixture over lettuce mixture; toss gently to coat. Arrange 1 cup salad on each of 6 plates; top each serving with 1 tablespoon Sweet Spiced Almonds. **YIELD:** 6 servings.

CALORIES 84; FAT 4.2g (sat 0.3g, mono 2.4g, poly 1.3g); PROTEIN 2g; CARB 11.2g; FIBER 3.8g; CHOL 0mg; IRON 1.1mg; SODIUM 123mg; CALC 47mg

Sweet Spiced Almonds

Store at room temperature in an airtight container for up to one week.

1	**cup sliced almonds**
1/3	**cup packed brown sugar**
1	**teaspoon ground cinnamon**
1/2	**teaspoon ground coriander**

1/2	**teaspoon ground cumin**
1	**large egg white, lightly beaten**
	Cooking spray

1. Preheat oven to 325°.

2. Combine almonds and next 4 ingredients in a small bowl. Stir in egg white. Spread mixture evenly onto a foil-lined baking sheet coated with cooking spray. Bake at 325° for 10 minutes. Stir mixture; bake an additional 15 minutes or until crisp. Transfer foil to a wire rack; cool almond mixture. Break almond mixture into small pieces. YIELD: 2 cups (serving size: 1 tablespoon).

CALORIES 27; FAT 1.5g (sat 0.1g, mono 1g, poly 0.4g); PROTEIN 0.8g; CARB 2.9g; FIBER 0.4g; CHOL 0mg; IRON 0.2mg; SODIUM 3mg; CALC 11mg

6 STRATEGIES TO
Fight Cravings

If you rarely enjoy a food you crave, you're more likely to go overboard when you finally do give in. Indeed, according to a Tufts study, people who occasionally give in to hankerings manage their weight most successfully. Try these healthful strategies.

1. EAT REGULARLY. Waiting too long between meals can turn normal hunger pangs into an out-of-control craving. It's hard to make a good choice when you're starving. Keep healthful options—energy bars, fat-free milk, even an almond butter- and-jelly sandwich—on hand to keep hunger in check.

2. DELAY GRATIFICATION. When a craving hits, slip your mind into rational gear by saying, "not now, maybe tomorrow." Saying "later" rather than "never" may help decrease the frequency of cravings.

3. KEEP IT REAL. Eating an apple isn't likely to satisfy a yen for chocolate. Instead, enjoy what you really want—in moderation. Research shows that each subsequent taste of a food is rated as less enjoyable than the previous taste. The first bite is always the best; the second bite, second best. If you eat half of what you'd normally want, your satisfaction rating will still be very high.

4. PRACTICE PORTION CONTROL. It's easy to overeat if you munch straight from a box of cereal or a bag of pretzels. Portion one-cup servings into zip top plastic bags so you won't eat to excess. After all, snacks are fine. The USDA Dietary Guidelines allow 100 to 300 of "discretionary" calories daily. An ounce of dark chocolate (142 calories) or 1.25 ounces of baked potato chips (166 calories) fall well within that range.

5. CHOOSE HIGH-QUALITY FOODS WITH NUTRITIONAL BENEFITS. Tapenade spread on a fresh baguette will offer salty-meaty flavor from the olives (as well as heart-healthy fatty acids) and tasty carbs from the bread. If chocolate is your weakness, go for gourmet dark chocolate, which offers beneficial antioxidants along with great flavor. If you want something creamy, try thick Greek yogurt drizzled with honey. You'll gain some calcium as well as the rich creaminess you crave.

6. KEEP A FOOD DIARY. Write down what you're feeling when you have a craving. It helps to transfer your feelings onto paper, and you may find you don't have to eat. Also note the types of food and the times you eat; look for patterns so you're not caught off guard. Address underlying issues such as boredom or stress, and you will likely minimize cravings. Anticipate what triggers a craving, and be better prepared with a healthful option.

Garden Salad with Citrus Vinaigrette

This salad holds well, so it is a fine side to bring to a cookout or pack with a lunch.

Vinaigrette:
- 3 tablespoons fresh orange juice
- 1½ tablespoons fresh lime juice
- 2½ teaspoons extra-virgin olive oil
- 2 teaspoons honey
- 1 teaspoon red wine vinegar
- ¼ teaspoon salt
- ⅛ teaspoon freshly ground black pepper

Salad:
- 1½ cups (1 x ¼–inch) julienne-cut zucchini
- 1½ cups (1 x ¼–inch) julienne-cut yellow squash
- 1 cup fresh corn kernels (about 2 ears)
- 2 tablespoons finely chopped red onion
- 1 tablespoon finely chopped fresh flat-leaf parsley
- 1 tablespoon finely chopped fresh basil

1. To prepare vinaigrette, combine first 7 ingredients, stirring with a whisk.

2. To prepare salad, combine zucchini and remaining ingredients in a large bowl. Add vinaigrette; toss well. Cover and chill.

YIELD: 4 servings (serving size: 1 cup).

CALORIES 101; FAT 3.4g (sat 0.5g, mono 2.2g, poly 0.5g); PROTEIN 2.6g; CARB 17.4g; FIBER 3.6g; CHOL 0mg; IRON 0.8mg; SODIUM 154mg; CALC 30mg

Spelt Salad with White Beans and Artichokes

Spelt (also called farro) is a high-protein grain with a mellow nutty flavor, and it provides an alternative to bulgur for those who have wheat allergies. (Bulgur is a good substitute if you do not have spelt for this dish.) This salad is nice chilled or at room temperature. Include a cluster of red grapes and crusty Italian bread in your bag.

1¼ cups uncooked spelt (farro), rinsed and drained
2½ cups water
⅓ cup chopped fresh mint
⅓ cup chopped fresh parsley
¼ cup minced red onion
3 tablespoons fresh lemon juice
2 tablespoons olive oil
¼ teaspoon salt
⅛ teaspoon freshly ground black pepper
1 (15-ounce) can navy beans, rinsed and drained
1 (14-ounce) can artichoke hearts, drained and chopped

1. Combine spelt and 2½ cups water in a medium saucepan; bring to a boil. Cover, reduce heat, and simmer 30 minutes or until tender and liquid is absorbed.

2. Combine cooked spelt, mint, and remaining ingredients in a large bowl, stirring well. Cover and store in refrigerator.

YIELD: 5 servings (serving size: 1 cup).

CALORIES 204; FAT 6.5g (sat 0.8g, mono 4g, poly 0.9g); PROTEIN 7.4g; CARB 30.7g; FIBER 4.9g; CHOL 0mg; IRON 3.2mg; SODIUM 437mg; CALC 40mg

Asian Green Bean Salad

Snow peas can be substituted for the green beans in this hearty salad, if you prefer.

Salad:
- 3 ounces uncooked linguine
- 1 pound green beans, trimmed
- 2 cups diagonally sliced celery
- 1 cup thinly sliced red bell pepper
- ½ cup (½-inch) slices green onions
- ⅓ cup chopped fresh cilantro

Dressing:
- ¼ cup rice wine vinegar
- ¼ cup low-sodium soy sauce
- 2 tablespoons dark sesame oil
- 2 teaspoons grated peeled fresh ginger
- ½ teaspoon sugar
- ¼ teaspoon freshly ground black pepper
- 3 garlic cloves, minced
- 1 red jalapeño pepper, seeded and finely chopped (about 1 tablespoon)

1. To prepare salad, break linguine in half. Cook pasta according to package directions, omitting salt and fat; add beans during last 3 minutes of cooking. Drain and rinse with cold water; drain. Place mixture in a large bowl. Stir in celery, bell pepper, onions, and cilantro.

2. To prepare dressing, combine vinegar and remaining ingredients in a small bowl; stir with a whisk until blended. Add to salad; toss well. Cover and chill. **YIELD:** 8 servings (serving size: 1 cup).

CALORIES 101; FAT 3.8g (sat 0.5g, mono 1.5g, poly 1.6g); PROTEIN 3g; CARB 14.9g; FIBER 3.1g; CHOL 0mg; IRON 0.8mg; SODIUM 282mg; CALC 42mg

INGREDIENT TIP: A Microplane® grater is ideal for grating fibrous fresh ginger. Simply peel the ginger first, and then run it across the grate over a small bowl to collect the pulp and juice.

Green Salad with Grilled Tempeh and Maple-Soy Vinaigrette

8 ounces organic tempeh, cut crosswise into ¼-inch slices
1 teaspoon butter, melted
¼ teaspoon salt
2½ tablespoons low-sodium soy sauce, divided
1½ tablespoons maple syrup, divided
4 cups trimmed arugula
4 cups baby spinach (about 3 ounces)
½ cup thinly sliced yellow bell pepper (about ½ medium)
¼ cup thinly sliced green onions (about 2)
2 tablespoons apple cider vinegar
1 teaspoon extra-virgin olive oil
Dash of ground red pepper
1 garlic clove, finely chopped

1. Lightly brush both sides of tempeh slices with butter; sprinkle with salt. Heat a grill pan over medium-high heat. Add tempeh slices in a single layer; cook 1 minute on each side or until tempeh begins to brown and grill marks appear. Remove from heat. Combine 1 tablespoon soy sauce and 1 tablespoon maple syrup; brush over both sides of tempeh while still warm. Let tempeh cool completely; cut slices into bite-sized pieces.
2. Combine arugula, spinach, bell pepper, and onions in a large bowl. Combine remaining 1½ tablespoons soy sauce, remaining 1½ teaspoons maple syrup, vinegar, oil, red pepper, and garlic in a small bowl; stir well with a whisk. Drizzle soy mixture over greens mixture; toss to coat. Place 2 cups salad on each of 4 plates; top each serving with ½ cup tempeh. Serve immediately. **YIELD:** 4 servings.

CALORIES 153; FAT 5.3g (sat 1.8g, mono 1.9g, poly 1.3g); PROTEIN 14g; CARB 13.8g; FIBER 5g; CHOL 3mg; IRON 3.2mg; SODIUM 521mg; CALC 155mg

CHOICE INGREDIENT: *Tempeh*

A fermented food, tempeh is made from partly cooked soybeans inoculated with spores of a friendly mold in a process resembling cheesemaking. The mold creates threads that bind the beans into a flat cake. Tempeh is blanched or frozen to slow fermentation and preserve active enzymes. It has a yeasty flavor and firm texture. Tempeh can be made with soybeans alone or a combination of soy and a grain, such as rice, barley, or quinoa. All-soy tempeh is highest in protein, has the most pronounced flavor, and is highest in fat. Good grilled, sautéed, pan-crisped, or braised, tempeh is sold at natural-foods stores and in some large supermarkets.

Top Five Salad Tools

In addition to measuring cups and spoons and a good pepper mill, there are a few go-to kitchen helpers that make salad prep a breeze.

CHEF'S KNIFE

The chef's knife (along with a cutting board) is the workhorse of any kitchen. It's ideal for chopping herbs, onions, garlic, fruits, and vegetables and for cutting boneless meats (it even cuts through small bones, such as those of chicken and fish), slicing and dicing, and general cutting tasks.

COLANDERS/STRAINERS

We use both metal and plastic colanders in varying sizes. A large colander works well for draining salad greens and rinsing vegetables. A small strainer is great for separating fruit juice or pulp from seeds. Mesh strainers are the most versatile because nothing can get through the holes except liquid.

PEELER

A peeler removes the skin from both vegetables and fruits. Select one with a comfortable grip and an eyer to remove potato eyes and other blemishes on vegetables and fruits. It's also handy for making Parmesan cheese shavings.

STAINLESS STEEL BOX GRATER

A box-style grater gives you a choice of hole sizes. Use the smaller holes for grating hard cheese and the largest holes for shredding foods such as cheddar cheese or carrots.

WHISKS

Whisks in assorted sizes are ideal for emulsifying vinaigrettes and mixing salad dressings. Whisks are available both in stainless steel and nylon; the nylon ones won't scratch nonstick surfaces.

Caribbean Shrimp Salad with Lime Vinaigrette

Everything except the avocado, because it turns brown, can be readied in advance and kept in separate containers, covered, and chilled.

4 cups chopped cooked shrimp (about 1½ pounds)

5 tablespoons seasoned rice vinegar, divided

2 tablespoons chili garlic sauce (such as Lee Kum Kee)

1½ tablespoons olive oil

1 tablespoon grated lime rind

¼ cup fresh lime juice (about 3 large limes)

½ teaspoon paprika

½ teaspoon ground cumin

2 garlic cloves, minced

Dash of salt

8 cups fresh baby spinach

1 cup chopped peeled mango (about 1 large)

1 cup julienne-cut radishes

¼ cup diced peeled avocado

½ cup thinly sliced green onions

2 tablespoons unsalted pumpkinseed kernels

1. Combine shrimp, 2 tablespoons vinegar, and chili garlic sauce in a large bowl; toss well. Cover and chill 1 hour.

2. Combine remaining 3 tablespoons vinegar, oil, and next 6 ingredients a small bowl, stirring with a whisk.

3. Place 2 cups spinach on each of 4 plates; top each serving with 1 cup shrimp mixture. Arrange ¼ cup mango, ¼ cup radishes, and 1 tablespoon avocado around shrimp on each plate. Top each serving with 2 tablespoons green onions and 1½ teaspoons pumpkinseed kernels. Drizzle each salad with 2 tablespoons vinaigrette. **YIELD:** 4 servings.

CALORIES 281; FAT 10g (sat 1.7g, mono 5.7g, poly 2.2g); PROTEIN 30.3g; CARB 18.4g; FIBER 3.6g; CHOL 252mg; IRON 6.3mg; SODIUM 879mg; CALC 126mg

Coconut Crab and Shrimp Salad

This fresh, colorful seafood salad also makes a terrific appetizer. For a spicier dish, add the jalapeño pepper seeds, or use two peppers.

Cooking spray
- ½ pound medium shrimp, peeled and deveined
- ½ teaspoon salt, divided
- 1 cup fresh or frozen corn kernels, thawed (about 2 ears)
- ⅓ cup finely chopped onion
- ⅓ cup chopped fresh cilantro
- ⅓ cup diced peeled avocado
- ½ pound lump crabmeat, drained and shell pieces removed
- 1 jalapeño pepper, seeded and chopped
- 3 tablespoons fresh lemon juice
- 2 teaspoons extra-virgin olive oil
- 6 cups torn Boston lettuce (about 3 small heads)
- ¼ cup flaked sweetened coconut, toasted

1. Heat a medium nonstick skillet over medium-high heat. Coat pan with cooking spray. Add shrimp and ¼ teaspoon salt; cook 4 minutes or until shrimp are done, turning once. Remove from pan. Coarsely chop shrimp.

2. Combine corn and next 5 ingredients in a medium bowl. Gently stir in shrimp.

3. Combine juice, oil, and remaining ¼ teaspoon salt, stirring with a whisk. Drizzle juice mixture over shrimp mixture; toss gently to coat. Divide lettuce among each of 4 plates; top with shrimp mixture. Sprinkle evenly with toasted coconut. YIELD: 4 servings (serving size: 1½ cups lettuce, about 1 cup salad, and 1 tablespoon coconut).

CALORIES 223; FAT 8.5g (sat 2.2g, mono 3.6g, poly 1.3g); PROTEIN 24g; CARB 16g; FIBER 3g; CHOL 124mg; IRON 3mg; SODIUM 613mg; CALC 94mg

Mediterranean Salmon Salad

Short pastas such as orzo generally cook faster than longer varieties. In a pinch, use canned drained wild sockeye salmon, flaked with two forks, in place of the fillets.

$^1/_2$ cup uncooked orzo
2 (6-ounce) salmon fillets (about 1 inch thick)
$^1/_4$ teaspoon salt
$^1/_4$ teaspoon dried oregano
$^1/_8$ teaspoon black pepper
Cooking spray
2 cups torn spinach

$^1/_2$ cup chopped red bell pepper
$^1/_4$ cup chopped green onions
4 kalamata olives, pitted and chopped
3 tablespoons fresh lemon juice
2 tablespoons crumbled feta cheese

1. Preheat broiler.

2. Cook pasta according to package directions, omitting salt and fat.

3. Sprinkle salmon evenly with salt, oregano, and black pepper. Place on a broiler pan coated with cooking spray. Broil 10 minutes or until fish flakes easily when tested with a fork or until desired degree of doneness. Let stand 5 minutes; break into bite-sized pieces with 2 forks.

4. Combine pasta, salmon, spinach, and remaining ingredients in a medium bowl; toss well. YIELD: 4 servings (serving size: 1 cup).

CALORIES 231; FAT 7.7g (sat 1.6g, mono 2.7g, poly 2.3g); PROTEIN 20.3g; CARB 19.3g; FIBER 1.8g; CHOL 49mg; IRON 1.3mg; SODIUM 310mg; CALC 56mg

You can't go wrong when choosing between seasonal fresh fish, such as yellowfin tuna and wild salmon. Both contain the same number of calories, but yellowfin tuna (sometimes referred to as "ahi") is less fatty, offers eight more grams of protein than wild salmon, and is prized for its mild but not fishy flavor. Although wild salmon contains more fat, it also has more heart-healthy omega-3 fatty acids.

Yellowfin Tuna (4$\frac{1}{2}$ ounces cooked)
- 177   calories
- 1.6   grams total fat
- 0.35   grams omega-3s
- 38   grams protein

Wild Salmon (4$\frac{1}{2}$ ounces cooked)
- 177   calories
- 5.5   grams total fat
- 1.35   grams omega-3s
- 30   grams protein

Chicken-Fruit Salad

Pack undressed greens and fruit separately, and then toss them together with the dressing just as you're ready to dig in.

1 (10-ounce) package Italian-blend salad greens (about 6 cups)

2 cups grilled chicken breast strips (such as Louis Rich; about 6 ounces)

1 cup blueberries

1 cup quartered strawberries

1 cup sliced banana

1 cup sliced peeled kiwifruit (about 3 kiwifruit)

2 tablespoons pine nuts, toasted

2 tablespoons herbed goat cheese

³/₄ cup raspberry dressing

1. Arrange 1¹/₂ cups salad greens on each of 4 plates. Divide remaining ingredients except raspberry dressing equally among 4 plates. Drizzle each serving with 3 tablespoons raspberry dressing. **YIELD:** 4 servings.

CALORIES 332; FAT 8.8g (sat 2.4g, mono 3.3g, poly 2.1g); PROTEIN 15.9g; CARB 53.3g; FIBER 5.9g; CHOL 32mg; IRON 2.7mg; SODIUM 699mg; CALC 114mg

Curried Chicken Salad with Apples and Raisins

Enjoy this fruit-studded chicken salad with whole-grain crackers, or spread it on whole-wheat bread for a sandwich. Use store-bought rotisserie chicken or the Grilled Lemon-Herb Chicken on page 40.

- ¼ **cup low-fat mayonnaise**
- 1 **teaspoon curry powder**
- 2 **teaspoons water**
- 1 **cup chopped skinless, boneless Grilled Lemon-Herb Chicken (about 4 ounces), page 40**
- ¾ **cup chopped Braeburn apple (about 1 small)**
- ⅓ **cup diced celery**
- 3 **tablespoons raisins**
- ⅛ **teaspoon salt**

1. Combine mayonnaise, curry powder, and water in a medium bowl, stirring with a whisk until well blended. Add Grilled Lemon-Herb Chicken, chopped apple, celery, raisins, and salt; stir mixture well to combine. Cover and chill. **YIELD:** 2 servings (serving size: about 1 cup).

CALORIES 222; FAT 5.4g (sat 0.9g, mono 1.7g, poly 2g); PROTEIN 17.5g; CARB 26.9g; FIBER 2.5g; CHOL 50mg; IRON 1.5mg; SODIUM 731mg; CALC 30mg

Tabbouleh with Chicken and Red Pepper

Use rotisserie or leftover chicken for this dish, if you like. If you're making the mixture a few hours or more in advance, store the cucumber and tomato separately, and add them close to serving time to keep the salad at its best. Serve with hummus and pita chips for a flavorful, Middle Eastern–themed light lunch.

$^1/_2$ cup uncooked bulgur	$^1/_2$ cup diced English cucumber
$^1/_2$ cup boiling water	$^1/_4$ cup minced fresh mint
$1^1/_2$ cups diced plum tomato	$1^1/_2$ tablespoons fresh lemon juice
$^3/_4$ cup shredded cooked chicken breast	1 tablespoon extra-virgin olive oil
$^3/_4$ cup minced fresh flat-leaf parsley	$^1/_2$ teaspoon salt
$^1/_2$ cup finely chopped red bell pepper	$^1/_4$ teaspoon freshly ground black pepper

1. Combine bulgur and $^1/_2$ cup boiling water in a large bowl. Cover and let stand 15 minutes or until bulgur is tender. Drain well; return bulgur to bowl. Cool.

2. Add tomato and remaining ingredients; toss well. **YIELD:** 4 servings (serving size: $1^1/_4$ cups).

CALORIES 150; FAT 4.7g (sat 0.8g, mono 2.9g, poly 0.7g); PROTEIN 11.2g; CARB 16.9g; FIBER 4.5g; CHOL 22mg; IRON 1.6mg; SODIUM 326mg; CALC 33mg

CHOICE INGREDIENT: *Bulgur*

Bulgur, perhaps best known in the Lebanese preparation tabbouleh (a salad of bulgur, parsley, and tomatoes), is used widely throughout the Mediterranean. This nutty whole grain can be used like brown rice in salads and pilafs, or simply cooked or steamed and drizzled with oil and sprinkled with chopped herbs. Mediterranean and Middle Eastern markets carry bulgur, or look for it in the grains section of large grocery stores.

Chicken Salad with Olive Vinaigrette

You can substitute 2 cups cooked chicken or turkey breast for vacuum-packed chicken.

1 cup uncooked Israeli couscous	1 tablespoon fresh lemon juice
¼ cup chopped pitted kalamata olives	¼ teaspoon salt
	¼ teaspoon freshly ground black pepper
2 tablespoons chopped fresh flat-leaf parsley	1 garlic clove, minced
1 tablespoon chopped capers	2 (7-ounce) packages 98% fat-free chicken breast in water
2 tablespoons extra-virgin olive oil	

1. Cook couscous according to package directions, omitting salt and fat. Drain and rinse with cold water.

2. Combine olives and next 7 ingredients in a large bowl, stirring with a whisk. Add couscous to olive mixture; toss gently to coat. Stir in chicken just before serving. YIELD: 4 servings (serving size: 1½ cups).

CALORIES 348; FAT 10.7g (sat 1.2g, mono 6.4g, poly 0.9g); PROTEIN 25g; CARB 34.9g; FIBER 2.4g; CHOL 18mg; IRON 1.9mg; SODIUM 929mg; CALC 66mg

> **QUICK TIP:** Add olives. Olives deliver big flavor, yet they're relatively low in calories (one serving of five kalamata olives contains about 25 calories). The olive bar at some supermarkets typically offers a variety, so try different types to mix things up.

Southwestern Chicken Pasta Salad

Fresh summer corn is sweet, tender, and juicy—cooked or raw.
If your corn is a bit past its prime, boil it for two minutes.

$\frac{1}{2}$ pound uncooked penne rigate
2 cups shredded skinless, boneless Grilled Lemon-Herb Chicken (about 8 ounces), page 40
1 cup fresh corn kernels
$\frac{3}{4}$ cup (3 ounces) shredded sharp cheddar cheese
$\frac{1}{2}$ cup sliced green onions
$\frac{1}{2}$ cup diced red bell pepper
$\frac{1}{2}$ cup chopped plum tomato (about 2 tomatoes)
$\frac{1}{4}$ cup fresh orange juice
2 tablespoons fresh lime juice
1 tablespoon extra-virgin olive oil
1 tablespoon chopped canned chipotle chiles in adobo sauce
$\frac{1}{2}$ teaspoon salt

1. Cook pasta according to package directions, omitting salt and fat. Drain and place in a large bowl. Add Grilled Lemon-Herb Chicken and next 5 ingredients; toss well to combine.
2. Combine orange juice and remaining ingredients, stirring with a whisk. Drizzle over pasta mixture; toss gently to coat. Cover and chill. **YIELD:** 6 servings (serving size: $1\frac{1}{3}$ cups).

CALORIES 322; FAT 9.9g (sat 3.6g, mono 3.8g, poly 1g); PROTEIN 21g; CARB 38.2g; FIBER 2.5g; CHOL 48mg; IRON 2.1mg; SODIUM 523mg; CALC 121mg

CHOICE INGREDIENT: Chipotles are dried smoked jalapeños that can also be found reconstituted and canned in a seasoned tomato sauce called adobo. Chipotle is a combination of the prefix *chi* (for "chile") and *potle* (Aztec word for "smoke"). Chipotles fall into the medium range of the heat index, with a smoky, slightly sweet, meaty, and savory flavor. Drying and smoking concentrates the jalapeño's heat. Chipotles in adobo are available in Latin markets and the ethnic aisle of most grocery stores.

Cuban Beans and Rice Salad

½ cup diced peeled avocado
2 tablespoons balsamic vinegar
1 tablespoon olive oil
1 teaspoon ground cumin
½ teaspoon salt
¼ teaspoon black pepper
3 cups cooked white rice
1 cup chopped, seeded plum tomato (about 3 tomatoes)
¼ cup minced fresh parsley
1 (15-ounce) can black beans, rinsed and drained
2 tablespoons minced fresh cilantro (optional)

1. Combine first 6 ingredients in a bowl, and toss gently. Add rice, next 3 ingredients, and cilantro, if desired; toss well. Serve chilled or at room temperature. **YIELD:** 6 servings (serving size: 1 cup).

CALORIES 184; FAT 4.6g (sat 0.7g, mono 3g, poly 0.5g); PROTEIN 4.9g; CARB 32.8g; FIBER 4g; CHOL 0mg; IRON 2.3mg; SODIUM 421mg; CALC 36mg

KITCHEN HOW-TO

International Guide to Spices

The first step in learning to cook any ethnic cuisine is to become familiar with that culture's seasonings. Study a culture's prevalent seasonings to add ethnic flavor to your cooking. Different cuisines tend to incorporate many of the same herbs and spices but in different combinations. Learn those, and you can add a little international flavor to your cooking.

Chinese Cuisine: aniseed, bean paste, chile oil, garlic, gingerroot, green onions, hot red peppers, sesame oil, sesame seeds, soy sauce, star anise

Mexican Cuisine: bell peppers, chiles, cilantro, cinnamon, cocoa, coriander seeds, cumin seeds, garlic, lime, onions, oregano, vanilla

German Cuisine: allspice, caraway seeds, cinnamon, dill, dill seeds, dry mustard powder, ginger, juniper berries, mustard seeds, nutmeg, onions, paprika, white pepper

French Cuisine: bay leaves, black pepper, chervil, chives, fines herbes, garlic, green and pink peppercorns, marjoram, nutmeg, onions, parsley, rosemary, shallots, tarragon, thyme

Caribbean Cuisine: allspice, cinnamon, cloves, coriander, curry, garlic, gingerroot, lime, nutmeg, onions, oregano, red pepper, Scotch bonnet peppers and hot sauce, thyme

Spanish Cuisine: almonds, bell peppers, cumin seeds, garlic, olives, onions, paprika, parsley, saffron

Italian Cuisine: anchovies, basil, bay leaves, fennel seeds, garlic, marjoram, onions, oregano, parsley, pine nuts, red pepper, rosemary

Scandinavian Cuisine: cardamom seeds, dill, dill seeds, lemon, mustard seeds, nutmeg, white pepper

Greek Cuisine: cinnamon, dill, garlic, lemon, mint, nutmeg, olives, oregano

Indian Cuisine: aniseed, black pepper, cardamom seeds, chiles, cilantro, cinnamon, cloves, coriander seeds, cumin seeds, curry powder, fenugreek (an aromatic Eurasian plant used in curry powder and other spice blends), garlic, gingerroot, mace, mint, mustard seeds, nutmeg, red pepper, saffron, sesame seeds, turmeric, yogurt

North African Cuisine: cilantro, cinnamon, coriander seeds, cumin seeds, garlic, gingerroot, mint, red pepper, saffron, turmeric

Grilled Lemon-Herb Chicken

1 (5-pound) roasting chicken
2 tablespoons chopped fresh parsley
1 tablespoon chopped fresh thyme

3 tablespoons fresh lemon juice
1 teaspoon salt
1/2 teaspoon freshly ground black pepper
Cooking spray

1. Remove and discard giblets and neck from chicken. Rinse chicken with cold water; pat dry. Trim excess fat. Place chicken, breast side down, on a cutting surface. Cut chicken in half lengthwise along backbone (do not cut through breastbone). Turn chicken over. Starting at neck cavity, loosen skin from breast and drumsticks by inserting fingers, gently pushing between skin and meat.

2. Combine parsley, thyme, juice, salt, and pepper; rub mixture under loosened skin and over breast and drumsticks. Gently press skin to secure. Place chicken in a large zip-top plastic bag. Seal and marinate in refrigerator 30 minutes.

3. Preheat grill to medium heat.

4. Place chicken, skin side up, on grill rack coated with cooking spray. Grill 55 minutes or until a thermometer inserted into meaty part of thigh registers 180°. Remove chicken from grill; cover and let stand 10 minutes. Remove and discard skin. **YIELD:** 5 servings (serving size: about 4 ounces meat).

CALORIES 203; FAT 6.2g (sat 1.7g, mono 2.2g, poly 1.4g); PROTEIN 33.5g; CARB 1.1g; FIBER 0.2g; CHOL 100mg; IRON 1.5mg; SODIUM 565mg; CALC 21mg

Ginger Beef Salad with Miso Vinaigrette

1 (1-pound) flank steak, trimmed
2 tablespoons minced peeled
   fresh ginger
¼ teaspoon salt
2 garlic cloves, minced
Cooking spray
2 tablespoons chopped fresh
   cilantro
2 tablespoons white miso
   (soybean paste)
2 tablespoons water
2 tablespoons rice vinegar

1 tablespoon canola oil
2 teaspoons grated peeled
   fresh ginger
½ teaspoon chile paste with
   garlic
6 cups torn Bibb lettuce (about
   3 small heads)
¾ cup thinly sliced yellow bell
   pepper
¼ cup thinly sliced red onion
½ English cucumber, halved
   lengthwise and sliced

1. Preheat broiler.

2. Sprinkle steak evenly with ginger, salt, and garlic. Place on a broiler pan coated with cooking spray; broil 6 minutes on each side or until desired degree of doneness. Let stand 5 minutes. Cut steak diagonally across grain into thin slices.

3. Combine cilantro and next 6 ingredients in a small bowl, stirring with a whisk. Combine lettuce and remaining ingredients in a large bowl. Drizzle half of miso mixture over lettuce mixture; toss to coat.

4. Place 1½ cups lettuce mixture on each of 4 plates. Top each with 3 ounces steak; top evenly with remaining miso mixture.

YIELD: 4 servings.

CALORIES 282; FAT 9.3g (sat 2.6g, mono 4.3g, poly 1.4g); PROTEIN 26.9g; CARB 22.9g; FIBER 3g; CHOL 37mg; IRON 3.2mg; SODIUM 708mg; CALC 57mg

Thai Pork Salad with Chili Dressing

Thai roasted red chili paste combines the kick of chili paste with a smoky flavor. If it is unavailable, chili paste with garlic or Sriracha is a good substitute.

2 ounces uncooked bean threads (cellophane noodles)

2 cups shredded napa (Chinese) cabbage

1½ cups thinly sliced seeded cucumber

1½ cups (¼-inch-thick) slices roasted pork (about 9 ounces)

1 cup thinly sliced red bell pepper strips

¾ cup finely shredded carrot

½ cup thinly sliced red onion

¼ cup thinly sliced fresh basil

¼ cup finely chopped fresh mint

1 serrano chile, seeded and finely chopped

¼ cup finely chopped green onions

3 tablespoons fresh lime juice

3 tablespoons seasoned rice vinegar

2 tablespoons sugar

1 tablespoon fish sauce

1 tablespoon roasted peanut oil

1½ teaspoons roasted red chili paste (such as Thai Kitchen)

¼ teaspoon salt

1. Pour boiling water over noodles; let stand 8 minutes or until tender. Drain and rinse with cold water. Drain. Snip noodles with kitchen shears. Combine noodles, cabbage, and next 8 ingredients in a large bowl, tossing gently. Combine green onions and remaining ingredients, stirring with a whisk. Pour green onion mixture over cabbage mixture; toss gently to coat.
YIELD: 6 servings (serving size: 1²/₃ cups).

CALORIES 231; FAT 5.7g (sat 1.3g, mono 2.5g, poly 1.4g); PROTEIN 11g; CARB 34.3g; FIBER 3.2g; CHOL 26mg; IRON 1 mg; SODIUM 861mg; CALC 61mg

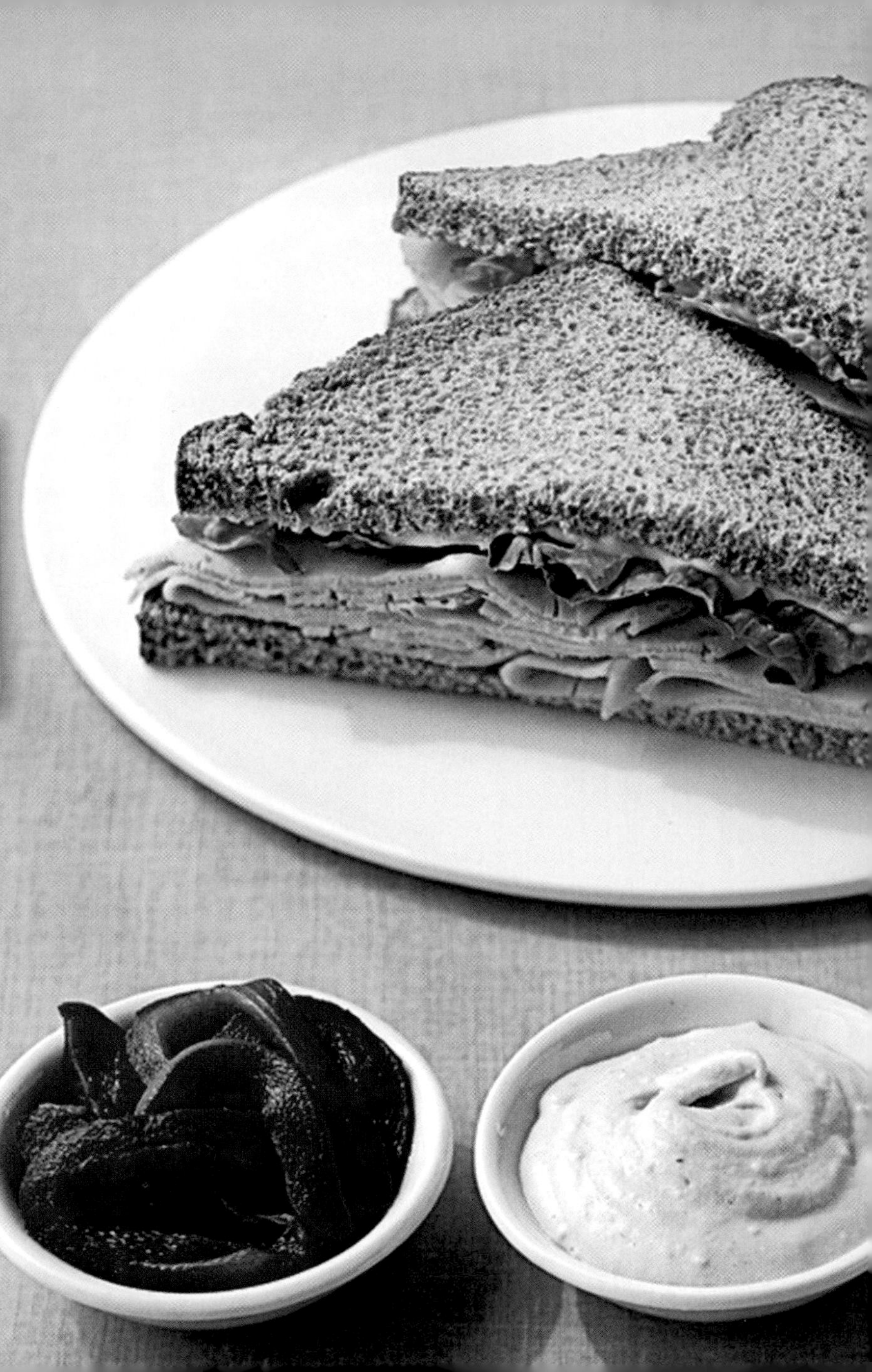

Hearty Sandwiches

Know How To Tote 'Em

Make what you can ahead.

Soups and stews improve with time, and dips and salsas often taste better once ingredients mingle, so plan ahead.

Keep things separate.

Prevent soggy sandwiches. Pack separate zip-top bags of tomato slices, lettuce, and bread, and then assemble the sandwiches just before serving. Know that some sandwiches are meant to absorb some liquid from the filling, so they can be assembled ahead of time. And don't dress leafy salads until you are ready to eat. Salt draws moisture out of watery ingredients, so add items such as tomatoes and cucumbers to a grain salad at the last minute for the best results.

Put leftovers to good use.

Consider incorporating some of tonight's dinner into tomorrow's lunch. Slice leftover chicken or beef and serve it on top of pasta or salad greens, mix it into a grain salad, or make it into a sandwich. Chop extra grilled vegetables and add them to soups, salads, or sandwiches.

Stay safe.

Keep cold food cold (below 40°) and hot food hot (above 140°) as it travels. Use insulated lunch bags, coolers, thermoses, ice bags, and frozen gel packs to help with temperature control. If reheating items in a microwave, the United States Department of Agriculture recommends they reach 165° and are served steaming hot.

With just a little organization and a few supplies, such as an insulated bag and serving-sized containers, your creative meals will make the trip. Try these four tips to ensure brown bagging success every time.

Roasted Red Pepper Spread Sandwiches

If you like pimiento cheese, you'll enjoy this recipe. Keep the sandwiches well chilled so that the cream cheese spread will remain firm. Sturdy, whole-grain bread works best.

½ cup finely chopped seeded cucumber	3 tablespoons minced red onion
1 (7-ounce) bottle roasted red bell peppers, drained and finely chopped	¼ teaspoon salt
	1 garlic clove, minced
¾ cup (6 ounces) ⅓-less-fat cream cheese, softened	8 (1½-ounce) slices whole-grain bread
⅓ cup (about 3 ounces) block-style fat-free cream cheese, softened	8 romaine lettuce leaves

1. Spread cucumber and bell peppers onto several layers of heavy-duty paper towels; let stand 5 minutes to drain excess moisture. Scrape into a medium bowl using a rubber spatula. Add cheeses, onion, salt, and garlic; stir with a fork until well blended. Spread about ½ cup cheese mixture over 4 bread slices; top each serving with 2 lettuce leaves and 1 bread slice. **YIELD:** 4 servings (serving size: 1 sandwich).

CALORIES 356; FAT 11.9g (sat 6.4g, mono 2.9g, poly 0.4g); PROTEIN 14.9g; CARB 43.6g; FIBER 4.1g; CHOL 36mg; IRON 2.9mg; SODIUM 875mg; CALC 173mg

Mr. Stripey Tomato, Arugula, and Pancetta Sandwiches

Try this new spin on the classic BLT. Pancetta is Italian cured bacon; substitute domestic cured bacon, if necessary. You can prepare the mayonnaise mixture and cook the pancetta up to one day ahead.

2 tablespoons light mayonnaise
1 tablespoon minced shallots
2 teaspoons Dijon mustard
½ teaspoon minced fresh sage
2 ounces pancetta, cut into 8 thin slices
   Cooking spray

8 (1-ounce) slices rustic sourdough bread, toasted
4 medium Mr. Stripey tomatoes, each cut into 4 (½-inch-thick) slices
1 cup arugula

1. Combine first 4 ingredients in a bowl, stirring well.

2. Preheat oven to 400°. Arrange pancetta in a single layer on a baking sheet coated with cooking spray. Bake at 400° for 8 minutes or until crisp. Drain on paper towels.

3. Spread mayonnaise mixture evenly over bread slices. Top each of 4 bread slices with 2 pancetta slices, 4 tomato slices, and ¼ cup arugula. Top sandwiches with remaining 4 bread slices. YIELD: 4 servings (serving size: 1 sandwich).

CALORIES 282; FAT 8.7g (sat 2.8g, mono 1.7g, poly 4.1g); PROTEIN 10.5g; CARB 41.9g; FIBER 3.5g; CHOL 13mg; IRON 3mg; SODIUM 699mg; CALC 44mg

Tuna Pan Bagnat

A favorite in southern France, *pan bagnat* (pan ban-YAH) means "bathed bread." The bread in this sandwich is meant to absorb some liquid from the filling, so it's great to make ahead of time.

- 1/3 cup finely chopped red onion
- 2 tablespoons chopped pitted niçoise olives
- 1 tablespoon fresh lemon juice
- 1/4 teaspoon kosher salt
- 1/4 teaspoon freshly ground black pepper
- 1 (6-ounce) can premium tuna, packed in oil, drained
- 1 hard-cooked large egg, chopped
- 1/4 cup thinly sliced fresh basil
- 2 teaspoons extra-virgin olive oil
- 1 (8-ounce) whole-wheat French bread baguette
- 1 garlic clove, halved
- 1 cup thinly sliced plum tomato (about 1)

1. Combine first 7 ingredients in a medium bowl. Combine basil and oil; stir with a whisk. Cut bread in half horizontally. Hollow out top and bottom halves of bread, leaving a 1-inch-thick shell; reserve torn bread for another use. Rub cut sides of garlic clove over cut sides of bread, and discard garlic. Drizzle basil mixture evenly over cut sides of bread. Spoon tuna mixture on bottom half of baguette. Arrange tomato slices over tuna mixture. Cover with top half of baguette. Wrap filled baguette in plastic wrap, and let stand 20 minutes. Cut filled baguette into 4 (3-inch) equal portions. **YIELD:** 4 servings (serving size: 1 sandwich).

CALORIES 248; FAT 9.3g (sat 1.4g, mono 4.6g, poly 2g); PROTEIN 14.5g; CARB 26.3g; FIBER 2.2g; CHOL 13mg; IRON 2mg; SODIUM 589mg; CALC 84mg

Tuscan Tuna Sandwiches

Chopped fennel bulb, fresh basil, and capers lend this speedy, no-cook supper vibrant Italian flair. Toasted bread adds a nice texture, but it's an optional step. You can serve the sandwiches with baked potato chips.

- $^1/_4$ cup finely chopped fennel bulb
- $^1/_4$ cup prechopped red onion
- $^1/_4$ cup chopped fresh basil
- 2 tablespoons drained capers
- 2 tablespoons fresh lemon juice
- 2 tablespoons extra-virgin olive oil
- $^1/_4$ teaspoon black pepper
- 2 (6-ounce) cans solid white tuna in water, drained
- 1 (4-ounce) jar chopped roasted red bell peppers, drained
- 8 (1-ounce) slices sourdough bread, toasted

1. Combine chopped fennel, red onion, $^1/_4$ cup basil, capers, lemon juice, olive oil, $^1/_4$ teaspoon black pepper, tuna, and bell peppers in a bowl, stirring well. Spoon $^1/_2$ cup tuna mixture on each of 4 bread slices. Top each serving with 1 bread slice. Cut each sandwich in half diagonally. **YIELD:** 4 servings (serving size: 1 sandwich).

CALORIES 292; FAT 10g (sat 1.6g, mono 5.6g, poly 1.7g); PROTEIN 25.2g; CARB 24.3g; FIBER 3.3g; CHOL 36 mg; IRON 2.4mg; SODIUM 878mg; CALC 85mg

CANNED TUNA: Three ounces of canned tuna contains approximately 50% of your daily vitamin D requirement. When buying canned tuna, keep the following in mind: The Food and Drug Administration (FDA)  recommends eating up to 12 ounces (or approximately two meals) of low-mercury fish per week as part of a healthy diet.

Lobster Rolls

One of the world's most luscious sandwiches, the lobster roll is an affordable way to stretch and enjoy this premium ingredient. The humble hot dog bun is traditional here, an important component that won't upstage the star. You can make the mayo-based lobster filling up to a day ahead and keep it refrigerated until just before serving.

5   tablespoons canola mayonnaise
1/4   cup finely chopped celery
3   tablespoons minced onion
2   tablespoons whole milk Greek-style yogurt (such as Fage)
1 1/2   teaspoons chopped fresh dill
1/2   teaspoon kosher salt

1/8   teaspoon ground red pepper
1   pound cooked lobster meat, cut into bite-sized pieces (about 3 (1 1/2-pound) lobsters)
2   tablespoons butter, melted
8   (1 1/2-ounce) hot dog buns
8   Bibb lettuce leaves

1. Combine first 7 ingredients in a medium bowl, stirring well. Add lobster to mayonnaise mixture; toss. Cover and chill 1 hour.
2. Brush butter evenly over cut sides of buns. Heat a large skillet over medium-high heat. Place buns, cut sides down, in pan; cook 2 minutes or until toasted. Line each bun with 1 lettuce leaf; top with 1/3 cup lobster mixture. YIELD: 8 servings (serving size: 1 sandwich).

CALORIES 272; FAT 12.3g (sat 3.3g, mono 5.1g, poly 2.9g); PROTEIN 16.3g; CARB 22.9g; FIBER 1.2g; CHOL 52mg; IRON 1.9mg; SODIUM 629mg; CALC 105mg

Feta-Basil Sandwiches

1 cup (4 ounces) crumbled
    feta cheese
1/4 cup chopped fresh basil
1/4 cup fat-free mayonnaise
1/4 teaspoon freshly ground
    black pepper

8 (1 1/2-ounce) slices firm white
    bread (such as Pepperidge Farm
    Hearty White), toasted
8 (1/4-inch-thick) slices tomato

1. Combine first 4 ingredients, tossing with a fork until well combined. Spread about 2 1/2 tablespoons cheese mixture onto each of 4 bread slices; top each sandwich with 2 tomato slices and 1 bread slice. **YIELD:** 4 servings (serving size: 1 sandwich).

CALORIES 313; FAT 9.6g (sat 4.3g, mono 2.7g, poly 0.9g); PROTEIN 14.4g; CARB 44.8g; FIBER 0.9g; CHOL 27mg; IRON 1.9mg; SODIUM 954mg; CALC 227mg

Little Italy Chicken Pitas

Use oil from the sun-dried tomatoes to prepare the vinaigrette for this zesty sandwich. Chilled green grapes are a cool side.

2 tablespoons balsamic vinegar	1 cup chopped tomato (about 1 medium)
1½ tablespoons sun-dried tomato oil	
1 tablespoon chopped drained oil-packed sun-dried tomatoes	½ cup (2 ounces) grated Asiago cheese
¼ teaspoon freshly ground black pepper	¼ cup thinly sliced fresh basil
1 garlic clove, minced	6 (6-inch) pitas, cut in half
4 cups shredded cooked chicken breast (about ¾ pound)	3 cups mixed baby greens

1. Combine first 5 ingredients in a large bowl. Stir in chicken, tomato, cheese, and basil. Line each pita half with ¼ cup greens. Divide chicken mixture evenly among pita halves. **YIELD:** 6 servings (serving size: 2 stuffed pita halves).

CALORIES 342; FAT 9.1g (sat 2.8g, mono 4.2g, poly 1.3g); PROTEIN 26.4g; CARB 37.3g; FIBER 2.4g; CHOL 56mg; IRON 2.7mg; SODIUM 397mg; CALC 162mg

Pineapple Chicken Salad Pitas

Almonds add crunch to the filling, though you can substitute toasted walnuts or pecans, if you prefer. Serve with a side of baked potato chips to round out the meal.

2½ cups chopped cooked chicken breast (about 1 pound)
½ cup matchstick-cut carrots
⅓ cup sliced almonds, toasted
⅓ cup light mayonnaise
¼ cup finely chopped green onions
¼ cup plain fat-free yogurt
1 tablespoon Worcestershire sauce
½ teaspoon garlic powder
¼ teaspoon salt
¼ teaspoon black pepper
1 (8-ounce) can crushed pineapple in juice, drained
4 (6-inch) whole-wheat pitas, each cut in half
8 romaine lettuce leaves

1. Combine first 11 ingredients in a large bowl, stirring well. Line each pita half with 1 lettuce leaf; fill each half with ⅓ cup chicken mixture. **YIELD:** 4 servings (serving size: 2 stuffed pita halves).

CALORIES 471; FAT 15.5g (sat 2.5g, mono 5.4g, poly 6.2g); PROTEIN 36.8g; CARB 48.8g; FIBER 7.2g; CHOL 82mg; IRON 3.9mg; SODIUM 776mg; CALC 98mg

Rosemary Chicken Salad Sandwiches

3 cups chopped roasted skinless, boneless chicken breast (about ³/₄ pound)
¹/₃ cup chopped green onions
¹/₄ cup chopped smoked almonds
¹/₄ cup plain fat-free yogurt
¹/₄ cup light mayonnaise
1 teaspoon chopped fresh rosemary
1 teaspoon Dijon mustard
¹/₈ teaspoon salt
¹/₈ teaspoon freshly ground black pepper
10 slices whole-grain bread

1. Combine first 9 ingredients, stirring well. Spread about ²/₃ cup chicken mixture over each of 5 bread slices, and top with remaining bread slices. Cut sandwiches diagonally in half.

YIELD: 5 servings (serving size: 1 sandwich).

CALORIES 360; FAT 11.6g (sat 2.1g, mono 3.5g, poly 1.8g); PROTEIN 33.6g; CARB 29.9g; FIBER 4.4g; CHOL 76mg; IRON 2.9mg; SODIUM 529mg; CALC 104mg

TAKE TWO: *Whole-Wheat Bread vs. Whole-Wheat Pita*

Either of these options can serve as a nutritional base for sandwiches, particularly when they are made with 100 percent whole wheat. Typically, two slices of whole-wheat bread contain fewer calories and a bit more fiber than one whole-wheat pita, which has less sodium. Both count as up to two of your three recommended daily servings of whole grain.

100% Whole-Wheat Bread (2 slices; 56 grams)
120 calories
250 milligrams sodium
4 grams fiber

100% Whole-Wheat Pita (1 pita; 55 grams)
140 calories
130 milligrams sodium
3 grams fiber

California Chicken Sandwiches

Citrus Mayonnaise:
- 1/3 cup fat-free mayonnaise
- 2 tablespoons thawed orange juice concentrate
- 1 teaspoon lime juice
- 1/2 teaspoon ground cumin
- 1/8 teaspoon hot sauce

Sandwiches:
- 4 (4-ounce) skinless, boneless chicken breast halves
- 1/4 teaspoon salt
- 1/8 teaspoon black pepper
- Cooking spray
- 8 (1 1/2-ounce) slices diagonally cut sourdough bread, toasted
- 4 small romaine lettuce leaves
- 2 plum tomatoes, each cut lengthwise into 4 slices
- 1 peeled avocado, cut into 8 wedges

1. To prepare citrus mayonnaise, combine first 5 ingredients in a small bowl.

2. To prepare sandwiches, sprinkle chicken with salt and pepper. Heat a large nonstick skillet over medium-high heat; coat pan with cooking spray. Add chicken. Cook 5 minutes on each side. Reduce heat to low. Cover; cook 5 minutes or until done. Remove from heat. Cut chicken diagonally across grain into thin slices.

3. Spread 1 tablespoon citrus mayonnaise on each of 4 bread slices. Top with 1 lettuce leaf, 1 chicken breast half, 2 tomato slices, 2 avocado wedges, and remaining bread slices. **YIELD:** 4 servings (serving size: 1 sandwich).

CALORIES 432; FAT 8.9g (sat 1.8g, mono 4.4g, poly 1.5g); PROTEIN 35.2g; CARB 53.8g; FIBER 2.8g; CHOL 66mg; IRON 3.7mg; SODIUM 951mg; CALC 112mg

CHOICE INGREDIENT: *Orange Juice Concentrate*

Orange juice concentrate adds intense citrus flavor to the mayonnaise without making the spread too thin. You don't have to thaw the whole container of concentrate to measure out 2 tablespoons. Allow it to stand at room temperature for about 15 minutes, and it will be soft enough to scoop out what you need. Then place the container in a zip-top plastic freezer bag, seal, and return the concentrate to the freezer. The remainder will be on hand for another recipe.

Buying Organic Food

History: The organic movement of the 60s and 70s was a reaction to growing awareness about the unintended environmental effects of chemical fertilizers and pesticides, which can spread far from the fields where they are applied. Today, organic farmers advocate maintaining a sustainable environment by using natural principles to maximize crop and livestock yield instead of turning to artificial and chemical methods.

USDA CERTIFICATION: The USDA has implemented uniform standards for American organic farmers and manufacturers. Organic foods must be grown or produced without chemical pesticides or fertilizers, and, in livestock, without the use of antibiotics or growth hormones. Organic foods cannot be genetically modified, irradiated, or cloned. Further guidelines govern specific foods. For instance, organic chickens must be raised with outdoor access.

GROWING MARKET: As organic farming has spread, it has adopted some of the principles that guide conventional farming. Today, some organic farms are large-scale operations that manage thousands of acres. As farming has grown, so have market share, crop yields, and distribution channels. Organic-themed grocery stores, such as Whole Foods, have expanded around the country, and even mainstream food purveyors, such as Safeway and Wal-Mart, have developed organic brands. Organic food can now be found in every corner of the grocery store.

GROWING COMPLEXITY: Today organic food may be locally grown, or it may be grown in a foreign country and shipped to the United States, resulting in a larger carbon footprint. Or it may be produced under less-than-ideal conditions for livestock or laborers. In response, some farmers are shifting to what is called "beyond organic" to practice sustainable farming, build a local clientele for foods raised in season, and provide a living wage to workers. Also, some farmers may follow organic principles yet forgo USDA certification. That's one reason why you sometimes find uncertified organic goods at your local grocery or farmers' market.

NUTRITION AND HEALTH: Farmers, food producers, and scientists debate whether organically grown and produced fruits, vegetables, meats, and milks are more nutritious than conventional ones. The Organic Center (TOC), a nonprofit research organization, recently issued a review of 97 studies on the subject to draw the conclusion that organic foods, on average, offer a 25 percent higher nutrient level over conventional ones. The premium may be an extra measure of a nutrient such as vitamin C or higher levels of antioxidants, which are produced by plants to act as natural pesticides.

Chicken Saté Wraps

Coconut milk, curry powder, and peanut butter bring Indonesian flair to a quick-fix sandwich.

Cooking spray
1/2 cup matchstick-cut carrots
1/3 cup chopped green onions
2/3 cup light coconut milk
1 tablespoon less-sodium soy sauce
1 tablespoon rice vinegar
3 tablespoons creamy peanut butter
1 teaspoon curry powder
1/8 teaspoon ground red pepper
2 cups shredded skinless, boneless rotisserie chicken breast
4 (8-inch) fat-free flour tortillas
1 1/3 cups packaged angel hair slaw

1. Heat a large nonstick skillet over medium-high heat. Coat pan with cooking spray. Add carrots and onions; sauté 1 minute. Stir in coconut milk and next 5 ingredients; cook 30 seconds, stirring constantly. Add chicken; cook 1 minute, stirring to coat. Remove from heat; cool. Warm tortillas according to package directions. Spoon about 1/2 cup chicken mixture down center of each tortilla, and top each with 1/3 cup angel hair slaw. Roll up. Cover and chill. **YIELD:** 4 servings (serving size: 1 wrap).

CALORIES 321; FAT 10.1g (sat 3.3g, mono 3.7g, poly 2.1g); PROTEIN 24.1g; CARB 25.5g; FIBER 4.3g; CHOL 49mg; IRON 0.9mg; SODIUM 844mg; CALC 37mg

Southwestern Steak, Corn, and Black Bean Wraps

You can use fresh corn in place of frozen; if it's fresh enough, it does not need to be cooked. To keep the wraps from getting soggy in the refrigerator, dole out the corn mixture with a slotted spoon. Try this with flavored tortillas to suit your taste.

1 cup frozen whole-kernel corn, thawed
$^1/_2$ cup chopped fresh cilantro
2 tablespoons minced red onion
2 tablespoons fresh lime juice
1 tablespoon extra-virgin olive oil
$^1/_2$ teaspoon ground cumin
$^1/_8$ teaspoon salt
$^1/_8$ teaspoon freshly ground black pepper
1 (15-ounce) can black beans, rinsed and drained
$2^1/_4$ cups chopped grilled flank steak (about 9 ounces)
6 (8-inch) fat-free flour tortillas
$^3/_4$ cup (3 ounces) shredded Monterey Jack cheese with jalapeño peppers

1. Combine first 9 ingredients, stirring well to coat. Arrange about $^1/_3$ cup flank steak down center of each tortilla. Top each tortilla with about $^1/_3$ cup corn mixture and 2 tablespoons cheese; roll up. Wrap sandwiches in aluminum foil or wax paper, and chill. **YIELD:** 6 servings (serving size: 1 wrap).

CALORIES 327; FAT 10.4g (sat 4.7g, mono 4.3g, poly 0.7g); PROTEIN 21g; CARB 39.8g; FIBER 4.6g; CHOL 37mg; IRON 3mg; SODIUM 796mg; CALC 131mg

Roast Beef and Blue Cheese Wraps

If blue cheese seems too strongly flavored, try Havarti or Muenster cheese. Wrap these sandwiches tightly in plastic wrap, and store in the refrigerator for up to a day.

³⁄₄ cup (3 ounces) crumbled blue cheese
2 tablespoons prepared horseradish
2 tablespoons low-fat mayonnaise
¹⁄₂ teaspoon freshly ground black pepper, divided
2 tablespoons sherry vinegar
1 tablespoon honey
1 garlic clove, minced
2 cups thinly sliced red cabbage
¹⁄₄ cup thinly sliced celery
¹⁄₄ cup thinly sliced fresh basil
3 (10-inch) flour tortillas
¹⁄₂ pound thinly sliced deli roast beef

1. Combine blue cheese, horseradish, mayonnaise, and ¹⁄₄ teaspoon pepper. Combine 1 tablespoon cheese mixture, vinegar, honey, and garlic in a medium bowl. Add ¹⁄₄ teaspoon pepper, cabbage, celery, and basil.

2. Warm tortillas according to package directions. Spread remaining cheese mixture evenly over tortillas. Divide beef and cabbage mixture evenly among tortillas; roll up. Cut each rolled tortilla in half crosswise. **YIELD:** 6 servings (serving size: 1 roll-up half).

CALORIES 241; FAT 7.7g (sat 3.6g, mono 2.5g, poly 0.6g); PROTEIN 13.5g; CARB 29.5g; FIBER 2.1g; CHOL 24mg; IRON 2.1mg; SODIUM 725mg; CALC 143mg

Beef, Orange, and Gorgonzola Sandwiches

Grilled flank steak with oranges and blue cheese combine in a sandwich that will make you the envy of coworkers when you open your lunch box. For the best results, use crusty rolls because they stay pleasantly crisp.

2 tablespoons cider vinegar
1½ teaspoons extra-virgin olive oil
½ teaspoon grated orange rind
⅛ teaspoon salt
⅛ teaspoon freshly ground black pepper
1 cup fresh orange sections (about 2 oranges)

4 (2-ounce) Italian or French rolls
2 cups thinly sliced grilled flank steak (about 8 ounces)
1 cup bagged prewashed baby spinach
¼ cup (1 ounce) crumbled Gorgonzola or other blue cheese

1. Combine first 5 ingredients, stirring with a whisk.

2. Pat orange sections dry with a paper towel. Slice each roll in half. Layer bottom of each roll with ½ cup flank steak, ¼ cup baby spinach, 1 tablespoon cheese, and ¼ cup orange sections. Drizzle each serving with about 2 teaspoons vinaigrette; top with top halves of rolls. Wrap in aluminum foil or wax paper; chill. YIELD: 4 servings (serving size: 1 sandwich).

CALORIES 318; FAT 10.2g (sat 4.6g, mono 3.7g, poly 0.5g); PROTEIN 21.6g; CARB 34.7g; FIBER 2.4g; CHOL 36mg; IRON 3.5mg; SODIUM 533mg; CALC 148mg

Chipotle Pork and Avocado Wraps

For a bit more spice in your wrap, add another teaspoon of chipotle chiles to the avocado spread.

$\frac{1}{2}$ cup mashed peeled avocado
$1\frac{1}{2}$ tablespoons low-fat mayonnaise
1 teaspoon fresh lime juice
2 teaspoons chopped canned chipotle chiles in adobo sauce
$\frac{1}{4}$ teaspoon salt
$\frac{1}{4}$ teaspoon ground cumin

$\frac{1}{4}$ teaspoon dried oregano
4 (8-inch) fat-free flour tortillas
$1\frac{1}{2}$ cups ($\frac{1}{4}$-inch-thick) slices roasted pork (about 8 ounces)
1 cup shredded iceberg lettuce
$\frac{1}{4}$ cup bottled salsa

1. Combine first 7 ingredients, stirring well.

2. Warm tortillas according to package directions. Spread about 2 tablespoons avocado mixture over each tortilla, leaving a 1-inch border. Arrange pork slices down center of tortillas. Top each tortilla with $\frac{1}{4}$ cup shredded lettuce and 1 tablespoon salsa, and roll up. **YIELD:** 4 servings (serving size: 1 wrap).

CALORIES 239; FAT 5.8g (sat 1.3g, mono 2.8g, poly 0.7g); PROTEIN 13.9g; CARB 32.8g; FIBER 2.6g; CHOL 29mg; IRON 1mg; SODIUM 683mg; CALC 27mg

Garlic-Rosemary Lamb Pitas

Stuff whole-wheat pitas with savory strips of lamb and a cool cucumber and yogurt tzatziki sauce for a fresh and flavorful meal from the Mediterranean. Try the recipe with chicken, too.

HEARTY SANDWICHES

2 teaspoons olive oil
1 tablespoon chopped fresh rosemary
1 teaspoon bottled minced garlic
1/2 teaspoon salt, divided
1/4 teaspoon black pepper
1 pound boneless leg of lamb, cut into (3/4-inch) cubes

1 1/2 cups finely chopped seeded cucumber
1 tablespoon fresh lemon juice
1/8 teaspoon black pepper
1 (6-ounce) container plain low-fat yogurt
4 (6-inch) whole-wheat pitas

1. Heat oil in a large nonstick skillet over medium-high heat. Combine rosemary, garlic, 1/4 teaspoon salt, 1/4 teaspoon pepper, and lamb, tossing to coat. Add lamb mixture to pan; sauté 4 minutes or until done.

2. While lamb cooks, combine 1/4 teaspoon salt, cucumber, lemon juice, 1/8 teaspoon pepper, and yogurt. Divide lamb mixture among each of 4 pitas, and drizzle with sauce. **YIELD:** 4 servings (serving size: about 3 ounces lamb, 1 pita, and 2/3 cup sauce).

CALORIES 391; FAT 11.5g (sat 3.5g, mono 4.8g, poly 1.5g); PROTEIN 32.7g; CARB 40.8g; FIBER 5.3g; CHOL 77mg; IRON 4.4mg; SODIUM 742mg; CALC 117mg

Lamb, Roasted Tomato, and Artichoke Sandwiches with Olive Spread

Roasting the tomatoes makes them sweet and meaty; it also draws out much of the liquid so that you can assemble the sandwiches the night before without worrying about the focaccia becoming soggy.

4 plum tomatoes, halved lengthwise (about ½ pound)
2 teaspoons olive oil
1½ teaspoons fresh thyme leaves, divided
¼ teaspoon freshly ground black pepper
¼ cup low-fat mayonnaise
2 tablespoons chopped ripe olives
1 tablespoon grated lemon rind

2 tablespoons fresh lemon juice
4 (2-ounce) pieces focaccia (Italian flatbread), cut in half horizontally
1¼ cups sliced roasted leg of lamb (about 6 ounces)
½ cup thinly sliced red onion
1 (14-ounce) can artichoke hearts, drained and thinly sliced

1. Preheat oven to 350°.

2. Arrange tomato halves, cut sides up, on a baking sheet. Drizzle with olive oil; sprinkle with 1 teaspoon thyme and black pepper. Bake at 350° for 45 minutes or until very tender. Cool slightly.

3. Combine remaining ½ teaspoon thyme, low-fat mayonnaise, olives, rind, and juice.

4. Spread cut sides of bread evenly with mayonnaise mixture. Divide tomato halves, lamb, onion, and artichokes evenly among 4 bread pieces. Top with remaining bread pieces. Wrap sandwiches in foil or parchment paper; chill. YIELD: 4 servings (serving size: 1 sandwich).

CALORIES 368; FAT 10.3g (sat 2.6g, mono 4.2g, poly 0.9g); PROTEIN 20.9g; CARB 49.9g; FIBER 5.9g; CHOL 39mg; IRON 3.1mg; SODIUM 831mg; CALC 24mg

Comfort Soups

Fresh Tomato Soup

2 cups fat-free, less-sodium chicken broth
1 cup chopped onion
¾ cup chopped celery
1 tablespoon thinly sliced fresh basil
1 tablespoon tomato paste
2 pounds plum tomatoes, cut into wedges
½ teaspoon salt
¼ teaspoon freshly ground black pepper
6 tablespoons plain low-fat yogurt
3 tablespoons thinly sliced fresh basil

1. Combine first 6 ingredients in a large saucepan; bring to a boil. Reduce heat, and simmer 30 minutes. Place half of tomato mixture in a blender. Remove center piece of blender lid (to allow steam to escape); secure blender lid on blender. Place a clean towel over opening in blender lid (to avoid splatters). Blend until smooth. Pour into a large bowl. Repeat procedure with remaining tomato mixture. Stir in salt and pepper. Ladle ¾ cup soup into each of 6 bowls; top each serving with 1 tablespoon yogurt and 1½ teaspoons basil. **YIELD:** 6 servings.

CALORIES 58; FAT 0.8g (sat 0.3g, mono 0.1g, poly 0.2g); PROTEIN 3.1g; CARB 11.3g; FIBER 2.8g; CHOL 1mg; IRON 1.1mg; SODIUM 382mg; CALC 49mg

PICK SEASONAL PRODUCE: When produce is in season and is plentiful, prices fall. But when it's out of season and there's less of it, we pay more. Moreover, out-of-season produce is often imported, which has another downside besides increased cost. Produce that has to be shipped thousands of miles has to be picked before it's ripe, which means you get less taste for your money. Find out what items are coming into peak season anytime of year by using CookingLight.com's In Season guide.

Cucumber Soup
The addition of avocado lends this soup a creamy touch.

11 large cucumbers (about 8 pounds), divided	2 teaspoons chopped fresh dill
¼ cup honey, divided	¼ teaspoon salt
¼ cup rice wine vinegar	¼ teaspoon freshly ground black pepper
1 ripe avocado, peeled and seeded	Cracked black pepper (optional)
	Dill sprigs (optional)

1. Cut 5 cucumbers into 3-inch chunks. Place half of cucumber chunks and 2 tablespoons honey in a blender or food processor; process until smooth. Pour pureed cucumber mixture through a cheesecloth-lined sieve into a bowl. Repeat procedure with remaining chunks. Cover and chill at least 8 hours.

2. Peel, seed, and thinly slice remaining 6 cucumbers; place slices in a bowl. Add vinegar and remaining 2 tablespoons honey; toss well to coat. Cover and chill 8 hours or overnight.

3. Working with pureed cucumber mixture in sieve, press mixture lightly with a wooden spoon or rubber spatula to squeeze out juice; discard solids.

4. Place half of marinated cucumber slices, avocado, and 1¾ cups cucumber juice in a blender or food processor; process until smooth. Pour cucumber mixture into a bowl. Repeat procedure with remaining cucumber slices and 1¾ cups cucumber juice; reserve any remaining juice for another use. Stir in chopped dill, salt, and pepper. Place 1½ cups soup into each of 6 bowls. Garnish with cracked black pepper and dill sprigs, if desired.

YIELD: 6 servings.

CALORIES 167; FAT 6g (sat 0.9g, mono 3.2g, poly 0.7g); PROTEIN 3.8g; CARB 27.3g; FIBER 5.3g; CHOL 0mg; IRON 1.6mg; SODIUM 312mg; CALC 79mg

Avocado Soup with Citrus-Shrimp Relish

This lovely no-cook soup makes a refreshing entrée with a green salad.

Relish:
- 2 tablespoons chopped fresh cilantro
- 1 teaspoon grated lemon rind
- 1 teaspoon finely chopped red onion
- 1 teaspoon extra-virgin olive oil
- 8 ounces peeled and deveined medium shrimp, steamed and coarsely chopped

Soup:
- 2 cups fat-free, less-sodium chicken broth
- 1³/₄ cups chopped avocado (about 2)
- 1 cup water
- 1 cup rinsed and drained canned navy beans
- ½ cup fat-free plain yogurt
- 1½ tablespoons fresh lemon juice
- ¼ teaspoon salt
- ¼ teaspoon black pepper
- ¼ teaspoon hot pepper sauce (such as Tabasco)
- 1 small jalapeño pepper, seeded and chopped
- ¼ cup (1 ounce) crumbled queso fresco cheese

1. To prepare relish, combine first 5 ingredients in a small bowl, tossing gently.

2. To prepare soup, place broth and next 9 ingredients in a blender; puree until smooth, scraping sides. Ladle 1¼ cups avocado mixture into each of 4 bowls; top each serving with ¼ cup shrimp relish and 1 tablespoon cheese. **YIELD:** 4 servings.

CALORIES 292; FAT 13.2g (sat 2.2g, mono 7.8g, poly 2.6g); PROTEIN 23.9g; CARB 22.5g; FIBER 7.3g; CHOL 118mg; IRON 3.4mg; SODIUM 832mg; CALC 146mg

CHOICE INGREDIENT: *Avocados*

Botanically, avocados are in fact a fruit, and if you have any doubt of their sweet flavor, try squeezing a lime over an avocado half and eating it with a spoon—it makes a great breakfast. This soup is thick and creamy, and a meal in itself with its topping of lemony shrimp, but it weighs in at less than 300 calories a bowl.

If you love the creamy, rich taste of avocados but worry about the fat and calorie content, we can put some of those fears to rest. While avocados are high in fat, most of it is "heart healthy" mono- and polyunsaturated fat. Concerned about calories? One-fifth of a medium-sized avocado has about 50 calories. Not bad considering these versatile fruits are nutrient-rich, containing nearly 20 vitamins and minerals. As long as you use moderation as your guide, avocados are a very nutritious and tasty addition to sandwiches, salads, and dips.

Golden Winter Soup

Leeks and potatoes provide the base for this hearty vegetable soup, and butternut squash adds a hint of sweetness.

2 tablespoons butter

5 cups ($\frac{1}{2}$-inch) cubed peeled butternut squash (about 1$\frac{1}{2}$ pounds)

2 cups ($\frac{1}{2}$-inch) cubed peeled russet potato (about 12 ounces)

1 teaspoon kosher salt

$\frac{1}{2}$ teaspoon freshly ground black pepper

2 cups sliced leek (about 2 medium)

4 cups fat-free, less-sodium chicken broth

1 cup half-and-half

12 ounces baguette, cut into 16 slices

$\frac{3}{4}$ cup (3 ounces) shredded Gruyère cheese

3 tablespoons chopped fresh chives

Freshly ground black pepper (optional)

1. Preheat broiler.

2. Melt butter in a large Dutch oven over medium-high heat. Add squash, potato, salt, and pepper to pan; sauté 3 minutes. Add leek; sauté 1 minute. Stir in broth; bring to a boil. Reduce heat, and simmer 20 minutes or until potato is tender, stirring occasionally. Place half of potato mixture in a blender. Remove center piece of blender lid (to allow steam to escape); secure blender lid on blender. Place a clean towel over opening in blender lid (to avoid splatters). Blend until smooth. Pour into a large bowl. Repeat procedure with remaining potato mixture. Stir in half-and-half. Cover and keep warm.

3. Arrange bread slices in a single layer on a baking sheet; sprinkle evenly with cheese. Broil bread slices 2 minutes or until golden. Ladle 1 cup soup into each of 8 bowls; top each serving with about 1 teaspoon chives. Serve 2 bread slices with each serving. Garnish with freshly ground black pepper, if desired. YIELD: 8 servings.

CALORIES 329; FAT 10.9g (sat 6.2g, mono 3g, poly 0.9g); PROTEIN 12.8g; CARB 46.7g; FIBER 4.8g; CHOL 30mg; IRON 3.2mg; SODIUM 813mg; CALC 217mg

Southwest Shrimp and Corn Chowder

2 tablespoons butter
1 cup chopped green onions
½ cup chopped red bell pepper
2 tablespoons finely chopped serrano chile (about 1 small)
1 (4.5-ounce) can chopped green chiles, undrained
3 tablespoons all-purpose flour
1½ cups 2% reduced-fat milk
1½ cups fat-free, less-sodium chicken broth
1½ cups frozen Southern-style hash brown potatoes, diced and thawed
½ teaspoon salt
½ teaspoon ground cumin
1 (15.25-ounce) can whole-kernel corn with red and green peppers, drained
1 pound peeled and deveined small shrimp
2 tablespoons chopped fresh cilantro

1. Melt butter in a large Dutch oven over medium-high heat. Add onions, bell pepper, and serrano chile to pan; sauté 2 minutes or until tender, stirring frequently. Add canned chiles to pan; cook 1 minute. Add flour to pan; cook 1 minute, stirring constantly. Stir in milk and next 5 ingredients; bring to a boil. Cook 5 minutes or until slightly thick. Stir in shrimp; cook 1 minute or until shrimp are done. Remove from heat; stir in cilantro. **YIELD:** 6 servings (serving size: about 1 cup).

CALORIES 212; FAT 6.7g (sat 3.4g, mono 1.5g, poly 0.7g); PROTEIN 19.3g; CARB 18.3g; FIBER 2.2g; CHOL 130mg; IRON 2.5mg; SODIUM 702mg; CALC 131mg

DESKTOP SNACK: Make the swap and choose nuts over chips for a crunchy alternative. Nuts are rich in heart-healthy fats but are calorically dense (about 170 calories per ounce), so measure out an ounce (about 24 almonds) and stick to that amount instead of feasting on the entire bag. Stash premeasured baggies of nuts in an office drawer or in your purse to nibble on when the 3 p.m. hunger pangs hit.

Cate's Springtime Risotto Soup

1 tablespoon olive oil
2 cups chopped onion
2 teaspoons grated lemon rind
¾ cup Arborio rice or other
   short-grain rice
3 (14 ½-ounce) cans fat-free,
   less-sodium chicken broth

2 cups (1-inch) sliced asparagus
   (about 1 pound)
2 cups coarsely chopped spinach
¼ teaspoon ground nutmeg
½ cup (2 ounces) grated fresh
   Parmesan cheese

1. Heat oil in a large saucepan over medium-high heat. Add onion; sauté 2 minutes.
2. Add lemon rind; sauté 2 minutes. Add rice; sauté 3 minutes.
3. Stir in broth, and bring to a boil. Cover, reduce heat, and simmer 10 minutes. Stir in asparagus, spinach, and nutmeg; cook, uncovered, 2 minutes or until asparagus is crisp-tender. Ladle soup into individual bowls, and top each serving with cheese. Serve immediately. **YIELD:** 4 servings (serving size: 1¾ cups soup and 2 tablespoons cheese).

CALORIES 320; FAT 7.5g (sat 2.9g, mono 3.6g, poly 0.5g); PROTEIN 14.9g; CARB 46.2g; FIBER 4.1g; CHOL 10mg; IRON 1.6mg; SODIUM 815mg; CALC 234mg

TAKE TWO: *Shrimp vs. Scallops*

Shrimp and scallops are great for a quick meal any time of the week. Either can be quickly sautéed and then added to salads, soups, and pastas, or served solo as an entrée or appetizer. Similar portions offer filling protein with relatively few calories and little fat. And each contains comparable sodium profiles—about 10 percent of your daily allotment and almost a day's worth of vitamin B12, a nutrient that helps support metabolism. However, a serving of shrimp yields about eight times as much iron (nearly one-fourth of a woman's daily needs).

SHRIMP (6 ounces): CALORIES 180; FAT 2.9g; PROTEIN 34.6g; IRON 4.1mg; SODIUM 252mg; 2.6 micrograms VITAMIN B_{12}

SCALLOPS (6 ounces): CALORIES 150; FAT 1.3g; PROTEIN 28.5g; IRON 0.5mg; SODIUM 274mg; 2.6 micrograms VITAMIN B_{12}

Thai Shrimp and Chicken Soup

The minced ginger, minced garlic, sliced mushrooms, and trimmed snow peas in this recipe require no preparation time at all. Find all those ingredients in your supermarket's produce department.

3 cups fat-free, less-sodium chicken broth
1 cup bottled clam juice
1 tablespoon fish sauce
2 teaspoons bottled minced garlic
1½ teaspoons bottled minced fresh ginger
¾ teaspoon red curry paste
1 (8-ounce) package presliced mushrooms
½ pound peeled and deveined large shrimp
½ pound skinless, boneless chicken breast, cut into 1-inch pieces

1 (3-ounce) package trimmed snow peas
¼ cup fresh lime juice
2 tablespoons sugar
2 tablespoons (½-inch) sliced green onion tops
2 tablespoons chopped fresh cilantro
1 (13.5-ounce) can light coconut milk

1. Combine first 6 ingredients in a large Dutch oven, stirring with a whisk. Add mushrooms; bring to a boil. Reduce heat, and simmer 4 minutes. Add shrimp, chicken, and snow peas; bring to a boil. Cover, reduce heat, and simmer 3 minutes.

2. Stir in lime juice and remaining ingredients. Cook 2 minutes or until thoroughly heated. **YIELD:** 4 servings (serving size: about 2 cups).

CALORIES 262; FAT 7.1g (sat 3.8g, mono 0.3g, poly 0.6g); PROTEIN 30g; CARB 18.3g; FIBER 1.8g; CHOL 121mg; IRON 3.3mg; SODIUM 973mg; CALC 64mg

Vietnamese Chicken Noodle Soup

Vietnamese cooking often calls for adding herbs and sauces to a dish at the end. More than just a garnish, these ingredients allow you to tailor the final product to your taste. Additional chili oil and fish sauce will, though, increase the fat and sodium.

4 cups water
1/2 cup sliced shallots
1/4 cup minced peeled fresh ginger
5 teaspoons minced garlic (about 2 large cloves)
1 tablespoon Thai fish sauce
1/2 teaspoon salt
1/2 teaspoon black pepper
2 (15.75-ounce) cans fat-free, less-sodium chicken broth
1 1/2 pounds skinless, boneless chicken thighs
1/4 pound uncooked rice sticks (rice-flour noodles) or vermicelli

1 cup fresh bean sprouts
2 tablespoons thinly sliced green onions
2 tablespoons chopped fresh cilantro
2 tablespoons thinly sliced fresh basil
2 tablespoons thinly sliced fresh mint
4 lime wedges
Chopped hot red or Thai chile (optional)
Fish sauce (optional)
Chili oil (optional)

1. Combine first 9 ingredients in a large Dutch oven; bring to a boil. Reduce heat, and simmer 15 minutes or until chicken is done. Remove chicken from pan; cool slightly. Cut into bite-sized pieces.

2. Cook rice sticks in boiling water 5 minutes; drain.

3. Divide chicken and noodles evenly among 4 large bowls. Ladle 2 cups soup into each bowl. Top each serving with 1/4 cup sprouts and 1 1/2 teaspoons each of onions, cilantro, basil, and mint. Serve with lime wedges; garnish with chopped chile, fish sauce, or chili oil, if desired. **YIELD:** 4 servings.

CALORIES 346; FAT 7.1g (sat 1.7g, mono 2.1g, poly 1.7g); PROTEIN 40.4g; CARB 29.1g; FIBER 1.1g; CHOL 141mg; IRON 2.6mg; SODIUM 1279mg; CALC 61mg

Thai basil (*rau que*; pronounced rao keh) is among the herbs that traditionally accompany Vietnamese dishes. The stems have a subtle purple hue.

Mung bean sprouts (*gia*; zia) have yellow tips and white stems, and add crunch to salads and soups. The stems have a subtle purple hue.

Lemongrass (*xa*; sa) adds tangy flavor to stir-fries, stews, and sauces. Remove the outer leaves and dark green leafy tops to reveal the creamy bulb, which can be chopped, crushed, sliced, or grated.

Fish sauce (*nuoc mam*; nyuk maam) is an indispensable seasoning made of anchovies. A good quality fish sauce really makes a difference; we like Three Crabs.

Chiles (*ot*; ut) vary widely in size and color. Very hot Thai or bird's-eye chiles are the most common.

Rice vermicelli (*banh hoai*; baan hoy) are thin rice noodles that are used in Vietnamese table salads.

Vietnamese Pantry

Many of these ingredients are available in the produce and ethnic food aisles at large supermarkets. You can also find them at Asian specialty markets.

Moroccan Chickpea Chili

This recipe proves you don't need meat to make a hearty chili.

2 teaspoons olive oil
1 cup prechopped onion
3/4 cup chopped celery
1/2 cup chopped carrot
1 teaspoon bottled minced garlic
2 teaspoons ground cumin
2 teaspoons paprika
1 teaspoon ground ginger
1/2 teaspoon ground turmeric
1/4 teaspoon freshly ground
black pepper
1/4 teaspoon salt
1/8 teaspoon ground cinnamon

1/8 teaspoon ground red pepper
1 1/2 cups water
2 tablespoons no-salt-added
tomato paste
2 (15 1/2-ounce) cans chickpeas
(garbanzo beans), rinsed
and drained
1 (14.5-ounce) can no-salt-added
diced tomatoes, undrained
2 tablespoons chopped fresh
cilantro
1 tablespoon fresh lemon juice

1. Heat oil in a large saucepan over medium-high heat. Add onion, celery, carrot, and garlic to pan; sauté 5 minutes. Stir in cumin and next 7 ingredients; cook 1 minute, stirring constantly. Add 1 1/2 cups water, tomato paste, chickpeas, and tomatoes; bring to a boil. Cover, reduce heat, and simmer 20 minutes. Stir in cilantro and juice. **YIELD:** 4 servings (serving size: 1 1/2 cups).

CALORIES 215; FAT 5.5g (sat 0.4g, mono 2.9g, poly 1.9g); PROTEIN 7.7g; CARB 36.3g; FIBER 9.8g; CHOL 0mg;
IRON 3.4mg; SODIUM 534mg; CALC 102mg

Butternut Squash Soup with Toasted Walnuts

This soup's delicious taste and creamy texture belie its simple preparation. Roasting the squash creates browned edges for a richer flavor.

8 cups (1-inch) cubed peeled butternut squash (about 2¼ pounds)
1½ teaspoons olive oil
¾ teaspoon salt, divided
½ teaspoon freshly ground black pepper, divided

Cooking spray
4 cups warm 2% reduced-fat milk, divided
1 (14-ounce) can fat-free, less-sodium chicken broth, divided
¼ cup chopped walnuts, toasted

1. Preheat oven to 400°.

2. Combine squash, oil, ¼ teaspoon salt, and ¼ teaspoon pepper on a foil-lined baking sheet coated with cooking spray. Bake at 400° for 45 minutes or until tender. Place half of squash, half of milk, and half of broth in a blender; process until smooth. Pour pureed mixture into a large saucepan. Repeat procedure with remaining squash, milk, and broth. Cook over medium heat 5 minutes or until thoroughly heated (do not bring to a boil). Stir in remaining ½ teaspoon salt and remaining ¼ teaspoon pepper. Ladle 1 cup soup into each of 8 bowls; sprinkle each serving with 1½ teaspoons nuts. YIELD: 8 servings.

CALORIES 204; FAT 5.9g (sat 1.9g, mono 1.7g, poly 2.1g); PROTEIN 7.5g; CARB 34.7g; FIBER 5.3g; CHOL 9mg; IRON 2mg; SODIUM 370mg; CALC 271mg

FREEZING TIPS: Most soups freeze well for up to two months. Pour them into airtight containers, leaving enough room for expansion (about 1 to 2 inches at the top of each container). To reheat, thaw in the refrigerator, place the contents in a saucepan, and reheat gently over low heat, adding some water or chicken broth, if necessary.

Black Bean Soup

1 cup dried black beans
2½ tablespoons extra-virgin olive oil, divided
¾ cup chopped onion
7 garlic cloves, minced and divided
2½ cups fat-free, less-sodium chicken broth
2 cups water
¼ cup no-salt-added tomato paste
1 teaspoon dried oregano
¾ teaspoon salt
¾ teaspoon ground cumin
¼ teaspoon ground red pepper
1 (4-ounce) can chopped green chiles
1 cup fresh cilantro leaves
½ jalapeño pepper, seeded
¼ cup crema Mexicana
3 hard-cooked large eggs, peeled and finely chopped
Cilantro leaves

1. Sort and wash beans, and place in a large Dutch oven. Cover with water; cover and let stand 8 hours. Drain beans.
2. Heat 1½ teaspoons oil in a Dutch oven over medium heat. Add onion; cook 4 minutes, stirring often. Add 5 garlic cloves; cook 1 minute. Increase heat to medium-high. Add beans, broth, and next 7 ingredients; bring to a boil. Cover, reduce heat, and simmer 1 hour or until beans are tender. Let stand 10 minutes.
3. Place half of bean mixture in a blender. Remove center piece of blender lid; secure blender lid on blender. Place a clean towel over opening in blender lid. Process until smooth. Pour into a large bowl. Repeat procedure with remaining mixture. Return soup to pan; cook 5 minutes, stirring often.
4. Finely chop 1 cup cilantro and jalapeño. Combine 2 tablespoons oil, 2 garlic cloves, cilantro, jalapeño, and crema. Ladle 1¼ cups soup into each of 4 bowls; top each with 2 tablespoons crema. Sprinkle soup with eggs. Garnish with cilantro leaves, if desired.
YIELD: 4 servings.

CALORIES 369; FAT 18.4g (sat 5.8g, mono 7.8g, poly 1.8g); PROTEIN 17.5g; CARB 34.7g; FIBER 11.8g; CHOL 173mg; IRON 4.8mg; SODIUM 829mg; CALC 114mg

Southwestern Chicken Soup

Although you can enjoy this soup with plain tortillas, it is also good with baked tortilla chips.

Cooking spray
1 cup chopped onion
3 garlic cloves, minced
6 cups fat-free, less-sodium chicken broth
1/4 cup uncooked white rice
1 teaspoon ground cumin
1 (16-ounce) can Great Northern beans, rinsed and drained
3 cups chopped skinless, boneless rotisserie chicken breast
1/2 cup coarsely chopped fresh cilantro
1/2 teaspoon black pepper
1/4 teaspoon salt
1 cup chopped seeded tomato
3/4 cup diced peeled avocado (about 1 medium)
1 tablespoon fresh lime juice
6 lime wedges

1. Heat a large sauté pan over medium-high heat. Coat pan with cooking spray. Add onion and garlic, and sauté 3 minutes. Add broth, rice, cumin, and beans; bring to a boil. Reduce heat; simmer 15 minutes. Stir in chicken, cilantro, pepper, and salt; simmer 5 minutes or until chicken is thoroughly heated.

2. Remove from heat, and stir in tomato, avocado, and juice. Serve with lime wedges. **YIELD:** 6 servings (serving size: 1²/₃ cups soup and 1 lime wedge).

CALORIES 274; FAT 7.7g (sat 1.5g, mono 3.9g, poly 1.3g); PROTEIN 28.4g; CARB 23.1g; FIBER 6g; CHOL 60mg; IRON 2.6mg; SODIUM 516mg; CALC 65mg

Corn and Bacon Chowder

To capture the freshness of yellow jewel-like corn without the fuss of shucking ears or cutting kernels off the cob, use packages of frozen baby gold and white corn. This chowder is so wonderfully sweet with the frozen corn that our taste testers gave it our highest rating.

2 bacon slices
1/2 cup refrigerated prechopped celery, onion, and bell pepper mix
2 (16-ounce) packages frozen baby gold and white corn, thawed and divided
2 cups 1% low-fat milk, divided
1/2 teaspoon salt
1/4 teaspoon freshly ground black pepper
3/4 cup (3 ounces) reduced-fat shredded extra-sharp cheddar cheese (such as Cracker Barrel)
Freshly ground black pepper (optional)

1. Cook bacon in a Dutch oven over medium heat until crisp. Remove bacon from pan; crumble and set aside. Add celery mixture and 1 package corn to drippings in pan; sauté 5 minutes or until vegetables are tender.
2. Place remaining 1 package corn and 1 cup milk in a blender, and process until smooth. Add pureed mixture to vegetables in pan; stir in remaining 1 cup milk, salt, black pepper, and cheese. Cook over medium heat (do not boil), stirring constantly, until cheese melts. Ladle chowder into bowls. Top each serving evenly with reserved crumbled bacon. Sprinkle with additional black pepper, if desired. **YIELD:** 6 servings (serving size: 1 cup).

CALORIES 215; FAT 6g (sat 3.1g, mono 1g, poly 0.6g); PROTEIN 10.8g; CARB 33.6g; FIBER 3.8g; CHOL 15mg; IRON 0.8mg; SODIUM 402mg; CALC 208mg

Brunswick Stew

Although traditional Brunswick stew is sometimes thickened with stale bread cubes, this version uses flour to give it body and features garlic bread on the side.

Cooking spray
1 cup chopped red bell pepper
¾ cup chopped yellow onion
½ cup chopped celery
1 tablespoon peanut oil
1 tablespoon all-purpose flour
1 pound skinless, boneless chicken thighs, cut into ½-inch pieces
2 cups fat-free, less-sodium chicken broth
2 tablespoons no-salt-added tomato paste

1 teaspoon dried thyme
½ teaspoon salt
½ teaspoon hot pepper sauce (such as Tabasco)
1 (10-ounce) package frozen whole-kernel corn, thawed
1 (10-ounce) package frozen baby lima beans, thawed
6 (1-ounce) slices Italian bread, toasted
2 garlic cloves, halved

1. Heat a large Dutch oven over medium-high heat. Coat pan with cooking spray. Add bell pepper, onion, and celery to pan; cook 5 minutes, stirring occasionally. Add oil to pan. Combine flour and chicken in a medium bowl, tossing to coat. Add chicken to pan; cook 2 minutes or until lightly browned. Gradually stir in broth; bring to a boil. Cook 1 minute or until slightly thick, stirring constantly. Add tomato paste and next 5 ingredients to pan. Cover, reduce heat, and simmer 30 minutes.

2. Rub bread slices with cut sides of garlic; discard garlic. Serve bread with stew. YIELD: 6 servings (serving size: 1 cup stew and 1 slice bread).

CALORIES 319; FAT 9.2g (sat 2.2g, mono 3.5g, poly 2.6g); PROTEIN 22.4g; CARB 38g; FIBER 5.8g; CHOL 50mg; IRON 3.2mg; SODIUM 596mg; CALC 58mg

Broccoli and Chicken Soup

If the broccoli florets are large, break them into smaller pieces at the stalk instead of chopping them; they'll cook more quickly. If you have leftovers, you will want to thin the soup with a little chicken broth or milk to the desired consistency.

Cooking spray
2 cups chopped onion
1 cup presliced mushrooms
1 garlic clove, minced
3 tablespoons butter
1.1 ounces all-purpose flour (about ¼ cup)
4 cups 1% low-fat milk
1 (14-ounce) can fat-free, less-sodium chicken broth
4 ounces uncooked vermicelli, broken into 2-inch pieces
2 cups (8 ounces) shredded light processed cheese (such as Velveeta Light)
4 cups (1-inch) cubed cooked chicken breast
3 cups small broccoli florets (8 ounces)
1 cup half-and-half
1 teaspoon freshly ground black pepper
¾ teaspoon salt

1. Heat a Dutch oven over medium-high heat. Coat pan with cooking spray. Add onion, mushrooms, and garlic to pan; sauté 5 minutes or until liquid evaporates, stirring occasionally. Reduce heat to medium; add butter to mushroom mixture, stirring until butter melts. Sprinkle mushroom mixture with flour; cook 2 minutes, stirring occasionally. Gradually add milk and broth, stirring constantly with a whisk; bring to a boil. Reduce heat to medium-low; cook 10 minutes or until slightly thick, stirring constantly. Add pasta to pan; cook 10 minutes. Add cheese to pan, and stir until cheese melts. Add chicken and remaining ingredients to pan; cook 5 minutes or until broccoli is tender and soup is thoroughly heated. **YIELD:** 10 servings (serving size: 1 cup).

CALORIES 317; FAT 12.3g (sat 6.8g, mono 2.9g, poly 0.9g); PROTEIN 27.5g; CARB 23.8g; FIBER 1.9g; CHOL 74mg; IRON 1.6mg; SODIUM 723mg; CALC 179mg

TAKE TWO: *Broccoli vs. Cauliflower*

A serving of steamed broccoli offers more than a day's worth of vitamin C as well as 15 percent of your daily fiber needs, vitamin A, and heart-healthy folate and potassium, all in a low-calorie package. A similar-sized serving of cauliflower offers a bit less nutrition but still supplies fiber and 14 percent of daily folate needs plus nearly a day's worth of vitamin C. Choose orange-hued cauliflower for about 25 times more vitamin A than the familiar white variety.

Broccoli (1 cup steamed)	**Cauliflower** (1 cup steamed)
44 calories	29 calories
5 grams fiber	3 grams fiber
123 milligrams vitamin C	55 milligrams vitamin C
505 milligrams potassium	176 milligrams potassium
94 micrograms folate	55 micrograms folate
114 micrograms vitamin A	1 microgram vitamin A

Beef and Barley Soup

Lamb may be used in place of chuck steak, if desired. Use one pound of boneless leg of lamb, cut into one-inch pieces.

Cooking spray
2 cups chopped onion (about 1 large)
1 pound chuck steak, trimmed and cut into $1/2$-inch cubes
$1^1/2$ cups chopped peeled carrot (about 4)
1 cup chopped celery (about 4 stalks)
5 garlic cloves, minced
1 cup uncooked pearl barley
5 cups fat-free, less-sodium beef broth
2 cups water
$1/2$ cup no-salt-added tomato puree
$1/2$ teaspoon kosher salt
$1/4$ teaspoon freshly ground black pepper
2 bay leaves

1. Heat a large Dutch oven over medium heat. Coat pan with cooking spray. Add chopped onion and beef to pan; cook 10 minutes or until onion is tender and beef is browned, stirring occasionally. Add chopped carrot and chopped celery to pan; cook 5 minutes, stirring occasionally. Stir in garlic; cook 30 seconds. Stir in barley and remaining ingredients, and bring to a boil. Cover, reduce heat, and simmer 40 minutes or until barley is done and vegetables are tender. Discard bay leaves. YIELD: 6 servings (serving size: $1^3/4$ cups)

CALORIES 275; FAT 5g (sat 1.6g, mono 2.3g, poly 0.5g); PROTEIN 21.8g; CARB 36g; FIBER 8g; CHOL 43mg; IRON 3.1mg; SODIUM 649mg; CALC 57mg

Provençal Beef Stew

Chuck roast, a tough cut of meat, becomes tender in the slow cooker. Serve this rustic stew with crusty bread.

2 teaspoons olive oil
1½ pounds boneless chuck roast, trimmed and cut into 1-inch cubes
1½ teaspoons kosher salt, divided
½ teaspoon freshly ground black pepper, divided
2 tablespoons all-purpose flour
2 medium onions, each cut into 8 wedges
8 garlic cloves, crushed
¼ cup dry red wine
1 cup fat-free, less-sodium beef broth
2 tablespoons tomato paste
3 bay leaves
3 fresh thyme sprigs
1 (14.5-ounce) can diced tomatoes, drained
3 cups (1-inch) slices zucchini
2 cups (1-inch) slices carrots

1. Heat oil in a large nonstick skillet over medium-high heat. Sprinkle beef with ½ teaspoon salt and ¼ teaspoon pepper; dredge in flour. Add beef to pan; sauté 2 minutes, browning on all sides. Place beef in an electric slow cooker. Add onions and garlic to pan; sauté 5 minutes. Add wine to pan, scraping pan to loosen browned bits. Place onion mixture in cooker. Add broth, tomato paste, bay leaves, thyme, and tomatoes to cooker; top with zucchini and carrots. Cover and cook on LOW 8 hours or until beef is tender. Stir in remaining 1 teaspoon salt and remaining ¼ teaspoon pepper. Discard bay leaves and thyme sprigs. YIELD: 6 servings (serving size: 1⅓ cups).

CALORIES 271; FAT 8.9g (sat 2.8g, mono 4.1g, poly 0.6g); PROTEIN 31.1g; CARB 16.5g; FIBER 3.5g; CHOL 86mg; IRON 4.2mg; SODIUM 739mg; CALC 57mg

Chunky Two-Bean and Beef Chili

Garnish with Monterey Jack cheese, chopped onion, chopped cilantro, and chopped tomato.

1 tablespoon canola oil, divided
Cooking spray
1½ pounds beef stew meat
¾ teaspoon salt
1½ cups chopped onion
½ cup chopped green bell pepper
1 tablespoon minced fresh garlic
2 teaspoons finely chopped jalapeño pepper
⅔ cup cabernet sauvignon or dry red wine
1½ tablespoons brown sugar
2 tablespoons tomato paste
1½ teaspoons ground ancho chile pepper
1 teaspoon dried oregano
1 teaspoon ground red pepper
½ teaspoon chili powder
¼ teaspoon ground cumin
¼ teaspoon ground coriander
⅛ teaspoon ground cinnamon
1 (28-ounce) can whole tomatoes, undrained and chopped
1 (15-ounce) can dark red kidney beans, rinsed and drained
1 (15-ounce) can hot chili beans

1. Heat 1 teaspoon oil in a large Dutch oven coated with cooking spray over medium-high heat. Sprinkle beef with salt. Place half of beef in pan; sauté 8 minutes or until browned. Remove from pan. Repeat procedure with remaining beef; remove from pan.

2. Add 2 teaspoons oil, onion, and bell pepper to pan, and sauté 3 minutes. Add garlic and jalapeño; sauté 1 minute. Add wine, scraping pan to loosen browned bits. Return beef to pan.

3. Stir in remaining ingredients; bring to a boil. Cover, reduce heat, and simmer 1½ hours or until beef is tender, stirring occasionally. **YIELD:** 6 servings (serving size: about 1⅓ cups).

CALORIES 390; FAT 11.4g (sat 3.2g, mono 4.8g, poly 1.1g); PROTEIN 31.3g; CARB 37.5g; FIBER 10.1g; CHOL 71mg; IRON 5mg; SODIUM 825mg; CALC 94mg

Tequila Pork Chile Verde

Fresh tomatillos come in papery husks, which peel off easily to reveal what looks like small green tomatoes. They have a tart lemony flavor and must be cooked before eating; a brief stewing will mellow the flavor while leaving some of the characteristic tang.

2 teaspoons canola oil
3 tablespoons yellow cornmeal
1 tablespoon ancho chile powder
1 pound pork tenderloin, trimmed and cut into $^3/_4$-inch pieces
2 cups coarsely chopped fresh tomatillos (about 12 ounces)
1 (14-ounce) can fat-free, less-sodium chicken broth
1 (4.5-ounce) can chopped mild green chiles, drained
1 jalapeño pepper, seeded and finely chopped
$^1/_2$ cup thinly sliced green onions
$^1/_4$ cup chopped fresh cilantro
2 tablespoons tequila
$^1/_4$ teaspoon salt

1. Heat oil in a large nonstick skillet over medium-high heat.
2. Combine cornmeal and chile powder in a medium bowl. Add pork, tossing to coat. Remove pork from bowl, reserving any remaining cornmeal mixture. Add pork to pan; sauté 5 minutes or until browned. Stir in remaining cornmeal mixture; cook 30 seconds, stirring constantly. Stir in tomatillos, broth, chiles, and jalapeño; bring to a simmer over medium-low heat. Cook 8 minutes or until tomatillos are tender. Stir in onions and remaining ingredients; simmer 1 minute. **YIELD:** 4 servings (serving size: 1$^1/_4$ cups).

CALORIES 245; FAT 7.4g (sat 1.7g, mono 3.3g, poly 1.6g); PROTEIN 26.5g; CARB 14.8g; FIBER 3.4g; CHOL 74mg; IRON 2.7mg; SODIUM 407mg; CALC 30mg

Sweet Endings

Blueberry-Orange Parfaits

This snack comes together in a few minutes if you purchase orange sections from the refrigerated part of the produce section. To make ahead, prepare parfaits and refrigerate, covered, for up to four hours; sprinkle with wheat germ just before serving.

1½ **tablespoons demerara or turbinado sugar**
 ½ **teaspoon grated orange rind**
  2 **(7-ounce) containers reduced-fat plain Greek-style yogurt**

  2 **cups fresh blueberries**
  2 **cups orange sections (about 2 large)**
 ¼ **cup wheat germ**

1. Combine first 3 ingredients in a small bowl, stirring until blended. Spoon ¼ cup blueberries into each of 4 tall glasses. Spoon about 2½ tablespoons yogurt mixture over blueberries in each glass. Add ¼ cup orange to each serving. Repeat layers with remaining blueberries, yogurt mixture, and orange. Sprinkle 1 tablespoon wheat germ over each serving; serve immediately.

YIELD: 4 servings (serving size: 1 parfait).

CALORIES 186; FAT 3g (sat 1.6g, mono 0.1g, poly 0.5g); PROTEIN 11.8g; CARB 31.9g; FIBER 4.2g; CHOL 5mg; IRON 1mg; SODIUM 34mg; CALC 125mg

CHOICE INGREDIENT: *Blueberries*

Of all the popular summer fruits, blueberries have a distinct advantage, nutritionally speaking. They've earned the distinction as one of the most potent sources of antioxidants, which help counteract heart disease, cancers, and other types of illnesses.

Blueberries are also full of fiber and high in vitamin C. To pick the best of the crop, look for powder-blue berries that are firm and uniform in size. Store them in a single layer, if possible, in a moisture-proof container for up to five days, and don't wash until you're ready to use them.

For out-of-season organic produce, try the frozen food case. When blueberries are no longer in season, you can buy organic berries that have been frozen at the peak of freshness and nutrition for half the price of fresh berries that have been flown in from far away.

Homemade Granola

6 cups rolled oats	¼ cup honey
¼ cup chopped almonds	¼ cup pineapple juice
¼ cup chopped pecans	½ teaspoon almond extract
2 tablespoons brown sugar	Cooking spray
¼ teaspoon kosher salt	¼ cup dried cranberries
⅓ cup maple syrup	¼ cup chopped dried apricots

1. Preheat oven to 300°.

2. Combine first 5 ingredients in a large bowl. Add syrup, honey, juice, and almond extract; toss well. Spread mixture evenly onto a jelly-roll pan coated with cooking spray. Bake at 300° for 45 minutes, stirring every 15 minutes. Stir in cranberries and apricots. Cool completely. Store in a zip-top plastic bag.

YIELD: 10 servings (serving size: ½ cup).

CALORIES 384; FAT 8.4g (sat 1.1g, mono 3.7g, poly 2.5g); PROTEIN 9.8g; CARB 68.1g; FIBER 7.8g; CHOL 0mg; IRON 3.4mg; SODIUM 52mg; CALC 57mg

Easy Lemon Squares

Crust:
- ¼ cup granulated sugar
- 3 tablespoons butter or stick margarine, softened
- 4.5 ounces all-purpose flour (about 1 cup)

Topping:
- 3 large eggs
- ¾ cup granulated sugar
- 2 teaspoons grated lemon rind
- ⅓ cup fresh lemon juice
- 3 tablespoons all-purpose flour
- ½ teaspoon baking powder
- ⅛ teaspoon salt
- 2 teaspoons powdered sugar

1. Preheat oven to 350°.

2. To prepare the crust, beat ¼ cup granulated sugar and butter with a mixer at medium speed until creamy. Weigh or lightly spoon 4.5 ounces flour into a dry measuring cup; level with a knife. Gradually add 4.5 ounces flour to sugar mixture, beating at low speed until mixture resembles fine crumbs. Gently press mixture into bottom of an 8-inch square baking pan. Bake at 350° for 15 minutes; cool on a wire rack.

3. To prepare topping, beat eggs at medium speed until foamy. Add ¾ cup granulated sugar and next 5 ingredients, and beat until well blended. Pour mixture over partially baked crust. Bake at 350° for 20 to 25 minutes or until set. Cool on wire rack. Sift powdered sugar evenly over top. **YIELD:** 16 servings.

CALORIES 118; FAT 3.2g (sat 1.7g, mono 1g, poly 0.3g); PROTEIN 2.2g; CARB 20.5g; FIBER 0.3g; CHOL 47mg; IRON 0.6mg; SODIUM 68mg; CALC 16mg

> **TIP:** For best results, bake these bars in an 8-inch square baking pan. Allow the lemon squares to cool completely in the pan on a wire rack before cutting them into bars. This will help ensure a "clean" cut. Finish with a light dusting of powdered sugar shaken through a sieve. Store in an airtight container between layers of wax paper in the refrigerator.

Maple-Pecan Snack Cake

Syrup in the cake batter and the frosting yields tasty results in this moist cake. Walnuts would also work well with the maple syrup's distinctive taste.

Cake:

1	cup maple syrup
1	cup reduced-fat sour cream
$^{1}/_{4}$	cup butter, melted
1	teaspoon vanilla extract
1	large egg
11.25	ounces all-purpose flour (about 2$^{1}/_{2}$ cups)
1	teaspoon baking soda
$^{1}/_{4}$	cup chopped pecans, toasted
$^{1}/_{2}$	teaspoon salt
	Cooking spray

Frosting:

1$^{1}/_{2}$	cups powdered sugar
2$^{1}/_{2}$	tablespoons maple syrup
1	tablespoon whipping cream
$^{1}/_{8}$	teaspoon salt
$^{1}/_{4}$	cup chopped pecans, toasted

1. Preheat oven to 350°.

2. To prepare cake, combine first 5 ingredients, stirring well with a whisk.

3. Weigh or lightly spoon flour into dry measuring cups; level with a knife. Combine flour, baking soda, $^{1}/_{4}$ cup pecans, and $^{1}/_{2}$ teaspoon salt in a large bowl, stirring with a whisk. Add syrup mixture to flour mixture; stir until well blended. Pour batter into a 9-inch square baking pan coated with cooking spray. Bake at 350° for 30 minutes or until a wooden pick inserted in center comes out clean. Cool completely on a wire rack.

4. To prepare frosting, combine sugar, 2$^{1}/_{2}$ tablespoons syrup, cream, and $^{1}/_{8}$ teaspoon salt. Beat with a mixer at medium speed until smooth. Spread frosting evenly over cooled cake; sprinkle with $^{1}/_{4}$ cup pecans. **YIELD:** 16 servings (serving size: 1 piece).

CALORIES 261; FAT 8.4g (sat 3.6g, mono 3.1g, poly 1.2g); PROTEIN 3.8g; CARB 43.2g; FIBER 0.9g; CHOL 27mg; IRON 1.4mg; SODIUM 208mg; CALC 44mg

Butterscotch Blondies

We wanted just enough salt to heighten the flavor, so we opted for unsalted butter. Browning the butter deepens its flavor and, when combined with brown sugar, creates the butterscotch taste.

9	ounces all-purpose flour (about 2 cups)	1/2	teaspoon salt
2 1/2	cups firmly packed light brown sugar	10	tablespoon unsalted butter
2	teaspoons baking powder	3/4	cup egg substitute
			Cooking spray

1. Preheat oven to 350°.

2. Weigh or lightly spoon flour into dry measuring cups; level with a knife. Combine flour, sugar, baking powder, and salt in a large bowl.

3. Place butter in a small skillet over medium heat. Cook 6 minutes or until lightly browned, stirring occasionally. Pour into a small bowl, and cool 10 minutes. Combine butter and egg substitute, stirring with a whisk. Pour butter mixture over flour mixture; stir just until moistened. Spoon batter into a 13 x 9-inch baking pan coated with cooking spray; smooth top with spatula. Bake at 350° for 30 minutes or until a wooden pick inserted in center comes out clean. Cool in pan on a wire rack. Cut into 48 squares. **YIELD:** 24 servings (serving size: 2 squares).

CALORIES 170; FAT 4.8g (sat 3g, mono 1.2g, poly 0.2g); PROTEIN 1.9g; CARB 30.5g; FIBER 0.3g; CHOL 13mg; IRON 1.1mg; SODIUM 108mg; CALC 45mg

Roasted Banana Bars with Browned Butter–Pecan Frosting

Bars:

- 2 cups sliced ripe banana (about 3 medium)
- 1/3 cup packed dark brown sugar
- 1 tablespoon butter, chilled and cut into small pieces
- 9 ounces cake flour (about 2 1/4 cups)
- 3/4 teaspoon baking soda
- 1/2 teaspoon baking powder
- 1/4 cup nonfat buttermilk
- 1 teaspoon vanilla extract
- 1/2 cup butter, softened
- 1 1/4 cups granulated sugar
- 2 large eggs
- Baking spray with flour

Frosting:

- 1/4 cup butter
- 2 cups powdered sugar
- 1/3 cup (3 ounces) 1/3-less-fat cream cheese, softened
- 1 teaspoon vanilla extract
- 1/4 cup chopped pecans, toasted

1. Preheat oven to 400°.

2. To prepare bars, combine banana, brown sugar, and 1 tablespoon butter in an 8-inch square baking dish. Bake at 400° for 35 minutes, stirring after 17 minutes. Cool slightly.

3. Reduce the oven temperature to 375°.

4. Weigh or lightly spoon cake flour into dry measuring cups; level with a knife. Combine 9 ounces (about 2¼ cups) flour, soda, and baking powder in a medium bowl. Combine banana mixture, buttermilk, and 1 teaspoon vanilla in another medium bowl. Place ½ cup butter and granulated sugar in a large bowl; beat with a mixer at medium speed until well blended. Add eggs to granulated sugar mixture; mix well. Add flour mixture to sugar mixture alternating with banana mixture, beginning and ending with flour mixture.

5. Pour batter into a 13 x 9–inch baking pan coated with baking spray. Bake at 375° for 20 minutes or until a wooden pick inserted in center comes out clean. Cool completely in pan on a wire rack.

6. To prepare frosting, melt ¼ cup butter in a small saucepan over medium heat; cook 4 minutes or until lightly browned. Cool slightly. Combine browned butter, powdered sugar, cream cheese, and 1 teaspoon vanilla in a medium bowl; beat with a mixer until smooth. Spread frosting over cooled bars. Sprinkle with pecans.

YIELD: 2 dozen (serving size: 1 bar).

CALORIES 221; FAT 8.4g (sat 4.7g, mono 2.3g, poly 0.6g); PROTEIN 2.3g; CARB 35.1g; FIBER 0.6g; CHOL 39mg; IRON 1mg; SODIUM 117mg; CALC 23mg

Chocolate Essentials

Chocolate is grown in the tropics near the equator. The biggest crops of cacao come from Brazil and the Ivory Coast in Africa. Cacao refers to the tree as well as its fruit and seeds.

Yellow-green grooved, oval fruit, about 12 inches long, grows directly from the trunk and lower branches of the tree. At harvest, the pods are cut from the trees, split open, and emptied of their 24 to 40 navy bean-sized seeds. The seeds are then fermented by heaping them into bins and covering from three to five days, during which they are shoveled and turned daily. Without proper fermentation, there is no possibility that the seeds, or cocoa beans, can be transformed into good chocolate later. After fermentation, the seeds are dried in the sun before they are bagged and shipped to chocolate factories. At the factory, the cocoa beans are cleaned, roasted, and winnowed to remove their hulls. Winnowing also breaks the hulled beans into pieces, called cocoa nibs. Nibs from different varieties and origins are usually blended after roasting to create different chocolates with distinct flavor characteristics, just as grapes are blended in making wine. After blending, the nibs are ground into chocolate liquor, which you know as unsweetened baking chocolate.

Storing Chocolate

Semisweet and bittersweet chocolate keep remarkably well for up to a year. Because chocolate absorbs flavors and odors, wrap in aluminum foil and again in plastic, and store it in a dry, cool place.

Milk and white chocolates lose freshness more quickly, so if you purchase more than you will use in two months, keep the extra frozen. Wrap with aluminum foil and plastic, and store in a zip-top bag. Before using frozen chocolate, thaw completely in the refrigerator without removing it from the bag. This will prevent condensation, which will damage the chocolate.

Chocolate-Mint Pudding

Fresh mint leaves steep in fat-free milk to impart the herb's essence; the taste is much better than that of mint extract. Unless milk is stabilized with a thickener such as flour or cornstarch, it will "break," or curdle, when it becomes too hot; that's why it's important to go no higher than 180° at the beginning of step one.

- 3 cups fat-free milk
- ½ cup packed fresh mint leaves (about ½ ounce)
- ⅔ cup sugar
- ¼ cup cornstarch
- 3 tablespoons unsweetened cocoa
- ⅛ teaspoon salt
- 3 large egg yolks, lightly beaten
- ½ teaspoon vanilla extract
- 2 ounces semisweet chocolate, chopped
- Mint sprigs (optional)

1. Heat milk over medium-high heat in a small, heavy saucepan to 180° or until tiny bubbles form around edge (do not boil). Remove from heat; add mint. Let stand 15 minutes; strain milk mixture through a sieve into a bowl, reserving milk. Discard solids. Return milk to pan; stir in sugar, cornstarch, cocoa, and salt. Return pan to medium heat; bring to a boil, stirring constantly with a whisk until mixture thickens.

2. Place egg yolks in a medium bowl; gradually add half of hot milk mixture, stirring constantly with a whisk. Add egg mixture to pan; bring to a boil, stirring constantly. Cook 1 minute or until thick. Remove from heat; add vanilla and chocolate, stirring until chocolate melts. Pour pudding into a bowl; cover surface of pudding with plastic wrap. Chill. Garnish with mint sprigs, if desired. **YIELD:** 6 servings (serving size: about ⅔ cup).

CALORIES 227; FAT 6.4g (sat 3.2g, mono 2.5g, poly 0.4g); PROTEIN 6.7g; CARB 39.4g; FIBER 1.2g; CHOL 105mg; IRON 1.1mg; SODIUM 106mg; CALC 173mg

Swag Bars

These no-bake bars come together quickly with common pantry ingredients. Make sure the cereal is well crushed (try packing it in a sealed zip-top plastic bag and using a rolling pin) so that it incorporates into the peanut butter mixture.

1³/₄ cups creamy peanut butter
³/₄ cup sugar
³/₄ cup light-colored corn syrup
1¹/₂ cups (6 ounces) chopped lightly salted, dry-roasted peanuts
3¹/₂ cups (4 ounces) whole-grain flaked cereal (such as Total), finely crushed

Cooking spray
¹/₃ cup (2 ounces) chopped dark chocolate

1. Combine first 3 ingredients in a heavy saucepan over medium-high heat. Cook 4 minutes or just until mixture begins to boil, stirring constantly. Remove from heat; stir in peanuts and cereal. Spread mixture evenly into a 13 x 9–inch baking pan coated with cooking spray.

2. Place dark chocolate in a small microwave-safe bowl. Microwave at HIGH 1 minute or until chocolate melts, stirring every 20 seconds. Drizzle chocolate evenly over peanut mixture. Score into 36 bars while warm. **YIELD:** 36 servings (serving size: 1 bar).

CALORIES 155; FAT 9.2g (sat 1.9g, mono 4.2g, poly 2.5g); PROTEIN 4.5g; CARB 16.2g; FIBER 1.5g; CHOL 0mg; IRON 2.3mg; SODIUM 121mg; CALC 113mg

Walnut Brittle

As the sugar mixture cooks, place the prepared jelly-roll pan in a 200° oven for about 10 minutes. This will help the sugar mixture stay warm and pliable so that you can spread it quickly and easily. The brittle is a good snack on its own, and we really like it crushed over low-fat vanilla ice cream.

Cooking spray
1 cup sugar
1 cup light-colored corn syrup
½ cup water
1 tablespoon butter
1½ cups coarsely chopped walnuts
1½ teaspoons baking soda
1 teaspoon vanilla extract

1. Line a jelly-roll pan with parchment paper, and coat paper lightly with cooking spray.

2. Combine sugar, light-colored corn syrup, ½ cup water, and butter in a heavy saucepan. Cook over medium heat, stirring until sugar dissolves. Cook 20 minutes or until a candy thermometer registers 275°. Stir in walnuts; cook 2 minutes or until candy thermometer registers 295°, stirring constantly. Remove from heat; stir in baking soda and vanilla (mixture will bubble). Quickly pour mixture onto prepared pan; spread to ¼-inch thickness using a wooden spoon coated with cooking spray. Cool completely; using a wooden spoon, break brittle into bite-sized pieces. **YIELD:** 24 servings (serving size: about 1 ounce).

CALORIES 125; FAT 5.4g (sat 0.8g, mono 0.8g, poly 3.6g); PROTEIN 1.2g; CARB 19.9g; FIBER 0.5g; CHOL 1mg; IRON 0.2mg; SODIUM 91mg; CALC 9mg

---

CHOICE INGREDIENT: *Walnuts*

Everyone thinks you have to eat salmon a couple of times a week to get the heart-healthy benefits of omega-3 fatty acids. A handful of walnuts will also give you a generous supply of this good fat. One ounce contains 2.5 grams of omega-3s, not to mention ample amounts of antioxidants, protein, and fiber. In fact, the FDA suggests that eating 1.5 ounces of walnuts a day as part of a diet low in saturated fat and cholesterol may reduce the risk of heart disease. The omega-3s' ability to reduce inflammation and clumping of platelets may have broad health implications for many chronic diseases facing us.

Ginger Cake

½ cup granulated sugar
½ cup applesauce
2 tablespoons canola oil
2 large eggs
1 cup molasses
6.75 ounces all-purpose flour (about 1½ cups)
½ cup flaxseed meal
½ cup toasted wheat germ
2 teaspoons baking soda
½ to 1 teaspoon ground cinnamon
½ to 1 teaspoon ground cloves
½ to 1 teaspoon ground ginger
¼ teaspoon salt
1 cup hot water
Cooking spray
1 tablespoon powdered sugar (optional)
Apple slices (optional)

1. Preheat oven to 350°.

2. Combine first 3 ingredients in a large bowl; beat with a mixer at medium speed until well blended (about 1 minute). Add eggs, 1 at a time, beating well after each addition. Stir in molasses.

3. Weigh or lightly spoon flour into dry measuring cups; level with a knife. Combine flour and next 7 ingredients in a large bowl. Add flour mixture and 1 cup hot water alternately to sugar mixture, beginning and ending with flour mixture. Spoon batter into a 13 x 9–inch baking pan coated with cooking spray. Bake 30 minutes or until a wooden pick inserted in center comes out clean. Cool in pan. Cut into 12 squares; sprinkle with powdered sugar, and serve with apple, if desired. **YIELD:** 12 servings (serving size: 1 square).

CALORIES 253; FAT 6.1g (sat 0.7g, mono 2.2g, poly 2.7g); PROTEIN 4.8g; CARB 46.1g; FIBER 2.6g; CHOL 35mg; IRON 2.9mg; SODIUM 284mg; CALC 81mg

SWEET ENDINGS

Garden Harvest Cake

Zucchini, carrot, and apples add moisture and flavor to quick breads, eliminating the need for excess butter and oil. It takes only about 10 minutes to prepare the batter for this simple cake. It's delicious for breakfast.

4.5 ounces all-purpose flour (about 1 cup)
3/4 cup sugar
2 teaspoons ground cinnamon
1 teaspoon baking soda
1/4 teaspoon salt
1/2 cup grated peeled Granny Smith apple (about 1 medium)
1/2 cup grated carrot (about 1 medium)
1/2 cup shredded zucchini
1/4 cup chopped walnuts, toasted
1/4 cup canola oil
1/4 cup nonfat buttermilk
2 large eggs
Cooking spray

1. Preheat oven to 350°.

2. Weigh or lightly spoon flour into a dry measuring cup; level with a knife. Combine flour and next 4 ingredients in a large bowl, stirring with a whisk. Add grated apple, grated carrot, shredded zucchini, and walnuts to flour mixture; toss well. Combine canola oil, buttermilk, and eggs in a small bowl, stirring with a whisk. Add egg mixture to flour mixture, stirring just until combined. Spoon batter into an 8 x 4-inch loaf pan coated with cooking spray. Bake at 350° for 50 minutes or until a wooden pick inserted in center comes out clean. Cool 10 minutes in pan on a wire rack; remove cake from pan. Cool completely on wire rack before slicing. **YIELD:** 9 servings (serving size: 1 slice).

CALORIES 223; FAT 9.7g (sat 1g, mono 4.4g, poly 3.6g); PROTEIN 3.8g; CARB 31.4g; FIBER 1.3g; CHOL 47mg; IRON 1.2mg; SODIUM 233mg; CALC 30mg

Texas Sheet Cake

Cooking spray
2 teaspoons all-purpose flour
9 ounces all-purpose flour (about 2 cups)
2 cups granulated sugar
1 teaspoon baking soda
1 teaspoon ground cinnamon
$^{1}/_{4}$ teaspoon salt
$^{3}/_{4}$ cup water
$^{1}/_{2}$ cup butter
$^{1}/_{2}$ cup unsweetened cocoa, divided
$^{1}/_{2}$ cup low-fat buttermilk
1 tablespoon vanilla extract, divided
2 large eggs
6 tablespoons butter
$^{1}/_{3}$ cup fat-free milk
3 cups powdered sugar
$^{1}/_{4}$ cup chopped pecans, toasted

1. Preheat oven to 375°.

2. Coat a 13 x 9-inch baking pan with cooking spray, and dust with 2 teaspoons flour. Set aside.

3. Weigh or lightly spoon 9 ounces flour into dry measuring cups; level with a knife. Combine 9 ounces flour and next 4 ingredients in a large bowl, stirring well with a whisk. Combine $^{3}/_{4}$ cup water, $^{1}/_{2}$ cup butter, and $^{1}/_{4}$ cup cocoa in a small saucepan; bring to a boil, stirring frequently. Add to flour mixture. Beat at medium speed with an electric mixer until well blended. Add buttermilk, 1 teaspoon vanilla, and eggs; beat well. Pour batter into prepared pan. Bake at 375° for 22 minutes or until a wooden pick inserted in center comes out clean. Place on a wire rack.

4. Combine 6 tablespoons butter, fat-free milk, and remaining $^{1}/_{4}$ cup cocoa in a saucepan; bring to a boil, stirring constantly. Remove from heat. Gradually stir in powdered sugar and remaining 2 teaspoons vanilla. Spread over hot cake. Sprinkle cake with pecans. Cool completely on wire rack. **YIELD:** 20 servings (serving size: 1 slice).

CALORIES 298; FAT 10g (sat 5.5g, mono 3.2g, poly 0.7g); PROTEIN 3.1g; CARB 49.8g; FIBER 0.5g; CHOL 44mg; IRON 1.1mg; SODIUM 188mg; CALC 25mg

Chocolate Shortbread

4.5 ounces all-purpose flour (about 1 cup)	1/2 cup powdered sugar
3 tablespoons unsweetened premium dark cocoa	5 tablespoons butter, softened
1/4 teaspoon salt	1/4 cup canola oil
	Cooking spray

1. Weigh or lightly spoon flour into a dry measuring cup; level with a knife. Combine flour, cocoa, and salt in a small bowl; stir with a whisk.

2. Place sugar, butter, and oil in a medium bowl; mix with hands until combined. Add flour mixture, and mix with hands until combined; wrap in plastic wrap. Refrigerate 30 minutes.

3. Preheat oven to 325°.

4. Place dough on a baking sheet coated with cooking spray; press dough into an 8 x 5–inch rectangle about 3/8-inch thick. Pierce entire surface liberally with a fork. Bake at 325° for 30 minutes or just until set. Cut shortbread into 24 pieces. Cool completely.

YIELD: 2 dozen (serving size: 1 cookie).

CALORIES 72; FAT 4.8g (sat 1.7g, mono 2.1g, poly 0.8g); PROTEIN 0.7g; CARB 7g; FIBER 0.3g; CHOL 6mg; IRON 0.3mg; SODIUM 42mg; CALC 2mg

Lemon Shortbread: A little bit of cornstarch ensures a short texture in the cookies. Substitute 3 tablespoons cornstarch for the unsweetened cocoa. Add 1/2 teaspoon grated lemon rind to flour mixture. Knead dough lightly 4 times or just until smooth before chilling. Bake 30 minutes or just until set and edges are golden.

CALORIES 74; FAT 4.8g (sat 1.7g, mono 2g, poly 0.8g); PROTEIN 0.6g; CARB 7.5g; FIBER 0.2g; CHOL 6mg; IRON 0.3mg; SODIUM 42mg; CALC 2mg

Double-Chocolate Cupcakes

These cupcakes are easy to make, and because simple ingredients are used, it's best to purchase premium cocoa powder and dark chocolate. A simple dusting of powdered sugar is enough to decorate these treats, which are studded with dark chocolate chunks. Bake them in muffin cup liners. A dozen of these are a terrific holiday treat to bring to coworkers at the office.

4.5 ounces all-purpose flour (about 1 cup)	$^1/_2$ cup egg substitute
$^1/_3$ cup unsweetened cocoa	1 teaspoon vanilla
1 teaspoon baking soda	$^1/_2$ cup 1% low-fat buttermilk
$^1/_8$ teaspoon salt	$1^1/_4$ ounces dark (70 percent cocoa) chocolate, finely chopped
$^2/_3$ cup granulated sugar	2 tablespoons powdered sugar
$^1/_4$ cup butter, softened	

1. Preheat oven to 350°.

2. Weigh or lightly spoon flour into a dry measuring cup, and level with a knife. Combine flour, cocoa, baking soda, and salt; stir with a whisk.

3. Place granulated sugar and butter in a large bowl; beat with a mixer at medium speed until well combined (about 3 minutes). Add egg substitute and vanilla, beating well. Add flour mixture and buttermilk alternately to granulated sugar mixture, beginning and ending with flour mixture. Fold in chocolate. Spoon batter into 12 muffin cups lined with muffin cup liners. Bake at 350° for 18 minutes or until cake springs back when touched lightly in center or until wooden pick inserted in center comes out clean. Remove from pan; cool completely on a wire rack. Sprinkle with powdered sugar just before serving. YIELD: 12 servings (serving size: 1 cupcake).

CALORIES 150; FAT 5.2g (sat 3.2g, mono 1.2g, poly 0.2g); PROTEIN 3.1g; CARB 24g; FIBER 1.1g; CHOL 11mg; IRON 1mg; SODIUM 125mg; CALC 42mg

Raspberry Cheesecake Bars

Line your pan with foil to easily remove and cut these bars. They are better if made the day before you serve them.

6.75 ounces all-purpose flour (about
    1¹/₂ cups)
³/₄ teaspoon salt
3¹/₂ tablespoons butter, melted
1 cup packed brown sugar
1¹/₂ teaspoons vanilla extract, divided
3 large eggs
¹/₂ cup granulated sugar
¹/₂ cup light sour cream
1 teaspoon grated lemon rind
1 tablespoon fresh lemon juice
1 (8-ounce) package ¹/₃-less-fat cream cheese
Cooking spray
1¹/₂ cups fresh raspberries

1. Preheat oven to 350°.

2. Weigh or lightly spoon flour into dry measuring cups; level with a knife. Combine flour and salt, stirring with a whisk.

3. Combine butter, brown sugar, 1 teaspoon vanilla, and eggs in a medium bowl, stirring with a whisk until smooth. Add flour mixture to butter mixture; stir just until moist.

4. Place ¹/₂ teaspoon vanilla, granulated sugar, and next 4 ingredients in a large bowl; beat with a mixer at high speed until fluffy.

5. Line a 13 x 9-inch baking pan with foil that extends 1 inch beyond sides; coat foil with cooking spray. Spread half of batter into pan. Pour cream cheese mixture over batter in pan, and spread evenly over batter. Sprinkle with raspberries. Drop remaining batter by tablespoonfuls over raspberries. Swirl batter, cream cheese mixture, and raspberries together with a knife.

6. Bake at 350° for 35 minutes or until a wooden pick inserted in center comes out clean. Cool completely on wire rack. Remove from pan by lifting foil. Remove foil; cut into 30 bar cookies.

YIELD: 30 servings (serving size: 1 cookie).

CALORIES 111; FAT 4g (sat 2.3g, mono 1.1g, poly 0.2g); PROTEIN 2.3g; CARB 16.9g; FIBER 0.6g; CHOL 32mg; IRON 0.6mg; SODIUM 113mg; CALC 23mg

TIPS FOR THE PERFECT CHEESECAKE

There are four ways to get graham cracker crumbs:

1. Buy boxed graham cracker crumbs; the work's already done for you!

2. Pulse graham crackers in a food processor until crumbs form.

3. Use a blender instead of a food processor; just do it in smaller batches, and make sure to pulse, not pulverize.

4. Place the graham crackers in a zip-top plastic bag, and crush by rolling with a heavy rolling pin or bottle to make crumbs.

Make sure that you're not scooping your flour. Follow our directions to lightly spoon the flour into a dry measuring cup, and then level off the excess with a knife. If you scoop, you can get up to twice as much flour as intended.

One medium lemon will give you 2 to 3 teaspoons of lemon rind. Be sure to wash the fruit prior to zesting. If you have it, use a citrus zester; otherwise, you can use a fine cheese grater. Only remove the colored part of the peel; the white portion is bitter.

If you don't have cheesecloth, you can line the colander with several layers of heavy-duty paper towels.

Because you're using a water bath to cook this cheesecake, line the outside of the springform pan with aluminum foil to prevent any water from seeping in.

The Perfect Cheesecake

½ cup graham cracker crumbs (about 6 cookie squares)	1 cup sugar
Cooking spray	2 teaspoons vanilla extract
1 (32-ounce) carton plain fat-free yogurt	1 tablespoon grated lemon rind
1.5 ounces all-purpose flour (about ⅓ cup)	⅓ cup fat-free sour cream
	2 (8-ounce) blocks ⅓-less-fat cream cheese, softened
	1 (8-ounce) carton egg substitute

1. Firmly press crumbs into the bottom and up the sides of a 9-inch springform pan coated with cooking spray.

2. Place a colander in a 2-quart glass measure or a medium bowl. Line the colander with four layers of cheesecloth, allowing cheesecloth to extend over outside edges of the bowl. Spoon yogurt into the colander. Cover loosely with plastic wrap, and refrigerate 12 hours. Spoon yogurt cheese into a bowl, and discard the liquid.

3. Preheat oven to 350°.

4. Weigh or lightly spoon flour into a dry measuring cup, and level with a knife. Combine drained yogurt, flour, and next 5 ingredients in a large bowl; beat at medium speed of a mixer until blended. Slowly add egg substitute, and beat until combined. Pour cheese mixture into prepared crust. Place in a large shallow baking pan, and add hot water to pan to a depth of 1 inch. Bake at 350° for 1 hour and 10 minutes. Remove sides from pan, and cool to room temperature. Cover and chill at least 8 hours. **YIELD:** 12 servings (serving size: 1 slice).

CALORIES 263; FAT 9.4g (sat 5.7g, mono 2.7g, poly 0.4g); PROTEIN 12.7g; CARB 30g; FIBER 0.1g; CHOL 29mg; IRON 0.8mg; SODIUM 264mg; CALC 224mg

Strawberries with Crunchy Almond Topping

This easy but stylish dessert is best made early in the day to let the strawberries macerate in the sweetened almond liqueur.

6 cups sliced strawberries	6 amaretti cookies, crushed
1/2 cup sugar	6 tablespoons reduced-fat
2 tablespoons amaretto (almond-flavored liqueur)	sour cream

1. Combine first 3 ingredients in a bowl. Cover and chill 4 to 8 hours. Spoon into individual dessert dishes. Sprinkle with crushed cookies; top with sour cream. **YIELD:** 6 servings (serving size: 1/2 cup strawberries, 1 crushed cookie, and 1 tablespoon sour cream).

CALORIES 207; FAT 2.6g (sat 0.4g, mono 0.3g, poly 0.3g); PROTEIN 2.8g; CARB 44g; FIBER 4.8g; CHOL 2mg; IRON 0.7mg; SODIUM 29mg; CALC 32mg

Simple Strawberry Mousse

2 cups quartered strawberries	1 1/2 cups frozen reduced-calorie
3 tablespoons sugar	whipped topping, thawed
1/2 cup low-fat sour cream	

1. Place strawberries and sugar in a blender, and process until smooth. Combine strawberry puree and sour cream in a large bowl, stirring well with a whisk. Fold whipped topping into strawberry mixture. Spoon into 6 (6-ounce) custard cups. Cover and freeze 4 hours or until firm. **YIELD:** 6 servings.

CALORIES 102; FAT 4.7g (sat 3.6g, mono 0.7g, poly 0.2g); PROTEIN 1.4g; CARB 14.5g; FIBER 1.2g; CHOL 8mg; IRON 0.2mg; SODIUM 20mg; CALC 40mg

Vanilla Bean Pudding

Vanilla beans can be expensive, but their superior flavor is worth the investment. Substitute vanilla paste or one teaspoon real vanilla extract if necessary. Stir extract in with the butter.

2$\frac{1}{2}$ cups 2% reduced-fat milk	$\frac{1}{8}$ teaspoon salt
1 vanilla bean, split lengthwise	$\frac{1}{4}$ cup half-and-half
$\frac{3}{4}$ cup sugar	2 large egg yolks
3 tablespoons cornstarch	4 teaspoons butter

1. Place milk in a medium, heavy saucepan. Scrape seeds from vanilla bean; add seeds and bean to milk. Bring to a boil.

2. Combine sugar, cornstarch, and salt in a large bowl, stirring well. Combine half-and-half and egg yolks, stirring well. Stir egg yolk mixture into sugar mixture. Gradually add half of hot milk to sugar mixture, stirring constantly with a whisk. Return hot milk mixture to pan; bring to a boil. Cook 1 minute, stirring constantly with a whisk. Remove from heat. Add butter, stirring until melted. Remove vanilla bean; discard.

3. Spoon pudding into a bowl. Place bowl in a large ice-filled bowl for 15 minutes or until pudding cools, stirring occasionally. Cover surface of pudding with plastic wrap; chill. **YIELD:** 6 servings (serving size: $\frac{1}{2}$ cup).

CALORIES 216; FAT 7.1g (sat 4.1g, mono 2.2g, poly 0.4g); PROTEIN 4.6g; CARB 34.2g; FIBER 0g; CHOL 86mg; IRON 0.2mg; SODIUM 125mg; CALC 142mg

Peanut Butter Pudding Variation: Omit vanilla bean, salt, and butter; stir in $\frac{1}{4}$ cup reduced-fat creamy peanut butter after custard is cooked. **YIELD:** 6 servings (serving size: about $\frac{1}{2}$ cup).

CALORIES 257; FAT 8.6g (sat 3.3g, mono 3.6g, poly 1.6g); PROTEIN 6.9g; CARB 39.2g; FIBER 0.7g; CHOL 80mg; IRON 0.5mg; SODIUM 170mg; CALC 142mg

Nutritional Analysis

How to Use It and Why Glance at the end of any *Cooking Light* recipe, and you'll see how committed we are to helping you make the best of today's light cooking. With chefs, registered dietitians, home economists, and a computer system that analyzes every ingredient, *Cooking Light* gives you authoritative dietary detail like no other magazine. We go to such lengths so you can see how our recipes fit into your healthful eating plan. If you're trying to lose weight, the calorie and fat figures will probably help most. But if you're keeping a close eye on the sodium, cholesterol, and saturated fat in your diet, we provide those numbers, too. And because many women don't get enough iron or calcium, we can also help there, as well. Finally, there's a fiber analysis for those of us who don't get enough roughage.

Here's a helpful guide to put our nutritional analysis numbers into perspective. Remember, one size doesn't fit all, so take your lifestyle, age, and circumstances into consideration when determining your nutrition needs. For example, pregnant or breast-feeding women need more protein, calories, and calcium. And men older than 50 need 1,200mg of calcium daily, 200mg more than the amount recommended for younger men.

In Our Nutritional Analysis, We Use These Abbreviations

sat	saturated fat	**CHOL**	cholesterol
mono	monounsaturated fat	**CALC**	calcium
poly	polyunsaturated fat	**g**	gram
CARB	carbohydrates	**mg**	milligram

Daily Nutrition Guide

	Women Ages 25 to 50	Women over 50	Men over 24
Calories	2,000	2,000 or less	2,700
Protein	50g	50g or less	63g
Fat	65g or less	65g or less	88g or less
Saturated Fat	20g or less	20g or less	27g or less
Carbohydrates	304g	304g	410g
Fiber	25g to 35g	25g to 35g	25g to 35g
Cholesterol	300mg or less	300mg or less	300mg or less
Iron	18mg	8mg	8mg
Sodium	2,300mg or less	1,500mg or less	2,300mg or less
Calcium	1,000mg	1,200mg	1,000mg

Metric Equivalents

The information in the following charts is provided to help cooks outside the United States successfully use the recipes in this book. All equivalents are approximate.

Liquid Ingredients by Volume

¼ tsp	=	1 ml					
½ tsp	=	2 ml					
1 tsp	=	5 ml					
3 tsp	=	1 tbl	=	½ floz	=	15 ml
2 tbls	=	⅛ cup	=	1 floz	=	30 ml
4 tbls	=	¼ cup	=	2 floz	=	60 ml
5⅓ tbls	=	⅓ cup	=	3 floz	=	80 ml
8 tbls	=	½ cup	=	4 floz	=	120 ml
10⅔ tbls	=	⅔ cup	=	5 floz	=	160 ml
12 tbls	=	¾ cup	=	6 floz	=	180 ml
16 tbls	=	1 cup	=	8 floz	=	240 ml
1 pt	=	2 cups	=	16 floz	=	480 ml
1 qt	=	4 cups	=	32 floz	=	960 ml
				33 floz	=	1000 ml	= 1l

Length

(To convert inches to centimeters, multiply the number of inches by 2.5.)

1 in	=			2.5 cm
6 in	=	½ ft	=	15 cm
12 in	=	1 ft	=	30 cm
36 in	=	3 ft = 1yd	=	90 cm
40 in	=			100 cm = 1m

Dry Ingredients by Weight

(To convert ounces to grams, multiply the number of ounces by 30.)

1 oz	=	¹⁄₁₆ lb	=	30 g
4 oz	=	¼ lb	=	120 g
8 oz	=	½ lb	=	240 g
12 oz	=	¾ lb	=	360 g
16 oz	=	1 lb	=	480 g

Cooking/Oven Temperatures

Fahrenheit	Celsius	Gas Mark
32° F	0° C	
68° F	20° C	
212° F	100° C	
325° F	160° C	3
350° F	180° C	4
375° F	190° C	5
400° F	200° C	6
425° F	220° C	7
450° F	230° C	8

Equivalents for Different Types of Ingredients

Standard Cup	Fine Powder (ex. flour)	Grain (ex. rice)	Granular (ex. sugar)	Liquid Solids (ex. butter)	Liquid (ex. milk)
1	140 g	150 g	190 g	200 g	240 ml
¾	105 g	113 g	143 g	150 g	180 ml
⅔	93 g	100 g	125 g	133 g	160 ml
½	70 g	75 g	95 g	100 g	120 ml
⅓	47 g	50 g	63 g	67 g	80 ml
¼	35 g	38 g	48 g	50 g	60 ml
⅛	18 g	19 g	24 g	25 g	30 ml

Index